A Year
of Ritual

About the Author

Sandra Kynes is an explorer of Celtic history, myth, and magic. Mainly a Hedge Druid, she is a member of the Order of Bards, Ovates, and Druids. She is a lay leader in a Unitarian Universalist congregation where her Samhain ritual has become a tradition. Her work with crystals, along with her interest in seeking connections between different cultures and practices, led her to devise the system of gemstone feng shui. In addition to the ritual-based program "Understanding the Language of the Goddess," which she created, Sandra also conducts wandmaking workshops. She has lived in England, Germany, and Massachusetts, but resided in New York City longer than any other place and considers it her hometown. Since 1997, her writings have been featured in Llewellyn's *Magical Almanac*, Llewellyn's *Spell-A-Day Calendar*, and Llewellyn's *Witches' Calendar* under the name Sedwyn.

To Write to the Author

If you wish to contact the author or would like more information about this book, please write to the author in care of Llewellyn Worldwide and we will forward your request. Both the author and publisher appreciate hearing from you and learning of your enjoyment of this book and how it has helped you. Llewellyn Worldwide cannot guarantee that every letter written to the author can be answered, but all will be forwarded. Please write to:

Sandra Kynes
℅ Llewellyn Worldwide
P.O. Box 64383, Dept. 0-7387-0583-7
St. Paul, MN 55164-0383, U.S.A.

Please enclose a self-addressed stamped envelope for reply,
or $1.00 to cover costs. If outside U.S.A., enclose
international postal reply coupon.

Many of Llewellyn's authors have websites with additional information and resources. For more information, please visit our website at http://www.llewellyn.com.

A Year of Ritual

Sabbats & Esbats
for Solitaries
& Covens

Sandra Kynes

2004
Llewellyn Publications
St. Paul, Minnesota 55164-0383, U.S.A.

First Edition
Second Printing, 2004

Book design and layout by Joanna Willis
Cover art © 2003 by Llewellyn art department
Cover design by Lisa Novak
Editing by Jane Hilken
Interior illustrations by Llewellyn art department

Library of Congress Cataloging-in-Publication Data
Kynes, Sandra, 1950–
   A year of ritual: Sabbats & esbats for solitaries & covens / Sandra Kynes.
      p.   cm.
   Includes bibliographical references and index.
   ISBN 0-7387-0583-7
    1. Sabbat. 2. Moon—Religious aspects. 3. Paganism—Rituals. 4. Religious calendars—
Neopaganism. 5. Witchcraft. I. Title.

  BF1572.S28K96 2004
  299'.94—dc22

                          2004048512

Llewellyn Publications
A Division of Llewellyn Worldwide, Ltd.
P.O. Box 64383, Dept. 0-7387-0583-7
St. Paul, MN 55164-0383, U.S.A.
www.llewellyn.com

Printed in the United States of America

This book is dedicated to

Balmardh, for his inspiration and challenge;

Charlene Dzielak, the Gaia of Gaia's Garden Grove
and someone who knows how to manifest a dream;

and Joe Dzielak, Charlene's beloved
who has gone ahead to the otherworld.

Contents

Introduction

*f*rom the Acropolis in Athens to Stonehenge on the Salisbury Plain and many other sites around the world, places of ritual are the most enduring signs of a civilization. In the underground Hal Saflieni Hypogeum on Malta and the long barrow of Newgrange in Ireland, rituals were held in tombs or tomblike places because in ritual one symbolically dies and surrenders oneself to the Divine. Because of the belief that death is followed by rebirth, ancient tombs also symbolically served as a womb. In the circle that we cast for ritual we temporarily re-create this tomb/womb that holds sacred energy. Like the ancient people reemerging from these places after ritual, when our circle is dissolved we are reborn to a new level of energy and consciousness.

In the workshop curriculum *Rise Up and Call Her Name*, Elizabeth Fisher noted that "to be in ritual is to be in the river of life."[1] To me this is a wonderful analogy because when you are physically in a river, your view of the world is very different from onshore. While in the river you can swim or simply go with the flow wherever the current may take you. The experience is refreshing and you feel different when you emerge. Unfortunately our fast-paced world equips us with blinders and we don't often look at things from a different perspective.

Modern life has become a blur. We go about our everyday tasks without noticing, much less making time for, things that could hold value for us. Ritual helps us to stop and see, to slow down and listen. It helps us regain and strengthen reverence for the natural world—the web of existence of which we are a part but that we so easily overlook.

During the Renaissance and so-called time of enlightenment, people began to gravitate toward the logic of science. Mysteries, including the mystery of life, became problems to be solved. In choosing to look at life as a technical issue, people began to lose their awe of the natural world. Nature became a thing to use and exploit. It became a commodity. In destroying the earth we destroy ourselves and it becomes a vicious cycle. If you feel awe and reverence for something, you do not destroy it.

Mystery is essential because it helps us find our place in the web of existence. This is important because we are not just physical and mental creatures (although one can go through life this way and be perfectly fine and happy). We are also spiritual creatures; we have this thing we call a soul (it is a mysterious thing) and for some of us we cannot shove it in a cabinet and keep it locked away. It will pound on the door for attention. We know that we must acknowledge this part of ourselves otherwise we are incomplete and we feel that there is a black hole at the center of our being. Ritual provides the means to hand ourselves over to spirit and to participate in the great dance of life.

When we enter into ritual we strengthen our connection with the cycles of nature. It brings us into rhythm with the natural world and with our own nature. When we take time to step outside of the mundane world, we encounter the rich flow of spiritual energy. We can reach deep inside ourselves and connect on a level that nourishes and gives us the strength to carry on in the rough-and-tumble of the physical and mental parts of our lives.

Entering sacred space helps us awaken to what is eternal within ourselves. When we do this, we also find where we fit in the web of life that surrounds us and touches everything in the universe. That connection also extends over time because as we engage in traditional celebrations with the sabbats, we connect ourselves with those who have gone before us, our ancestors. In a sense we also project out to the future to those who will follow in our footsteps. Our energy becomes part of a spiral that stretches through time and space.

After ritual, that part of us that we awakened cannot be stuffed into a box to await the next ritual. The energy that we raise changes us slightly each time so that when we go back into the world at large and pick up our mundane lives, we take some of the energy, some of the magic with us. In turn, it has an effect on the world around us like a ripple that spreads reverence and joy. It begins to run like a leitmotif through our lives. After experiencing our primal presence in ritual we begin to flow with a vitality that keeps the flame of spirit kindled within our hearts.

In a group, even if you do not have a Priest or Priestess role, ritual is not a passive event. Through ritual we learn that we are transformed and we become transformers. As the chant suggests, "we are the weavers, we are the web"; we realize that we can weave and transform our lives.

In the 1960s, biologist and educator Barry Commoner presented the four informal laws of ecology, which were almost immediately adopted by others as the four laws of energy. These can easily be applied to ritual:

- **Law 1: Everything is connected to everything else.** In ritual we feel this connection as we find our place in the web of existence. When we use magic we must be aware of its potential larger ramifications. As Ursula Le Guin noted, "To light a candle is to cast a shadow."[2]

- **Law 2: Everything must go somewhere.** Energy is in constant motion but it cannot be exerted in one direction indefinitely or it begins to deteriorate. Balance is essential. When we raise energy in ritual, we send it out to complete its purpose and then we ground any that is left over. Similarly, if we sense negative energy around us, rather than deflecting it back to its source (no matter where that may be), it is better to send it to the ground where the earth can neutralize it, preventing it from bouncing around and causing harm.

- **Law 3: Nature knows best.** Any Pagan would agree with this law. To me this means that the natural world has a wealth of knowledge that we have barely gotten our minds around. It also means that we need to learn when to "go with the flow" and when to "let nature take her course."

- **Law 4: There's no such thing as a free lunch.** It takes energy to raise energy; we cannot receive without giving. In ritual we expend energy on all levels: physical, mental, and spiritual in order to do magic or to reach deeper levels within our souls. We need to take care to replenish our energy and learn to tap into that unlimited, infinite universal source.

Types of Ritual

In addition to the sabbats and esbats that celebrate traditional events (more on these in their respective sections), we use ritual to mark events in our lives. By doing this, we make these occasions more meaningful. Each time we step out of the ordinary and into the sacred we have a chance to open our eyes and behold the fabric of our lives. Marking certain occasions with a ritual enriches that event. These special occasions may include:

- **Initiation:** This can be a ritual of acceptance into a tradition or a ritual to dedicate yourself to a path. It can be a group or solo ritual.

- **Handfasting:** This marks the joining of two people in marriage or union.

- **Birth or naming:** It is important to welcome a child into the physical world and to let him or her feel the bright circle of life. This ritual is sometimes called a "Wiccaning."

- **Coming of age:** It is an important rite of passage for children as they become young women and men to accept them into adulthood.

- **Croning:** Many older women feel the importance of marking their entrance into the third stage of life. Unlike the messages from the mainstream culture that adores youth, acknowledging that you are a wise woman is a step toward becoming one.

- **Death and passing over:** Because life is cyclical and not linear, death is not a mournful triumph over life. While it is sad to say good-bye, it is important to celebrate that person's life and how he or she may have touched yours.

Many other personal events are worth marking with ritual. Once we do this we find that life itself, despite all its ups and downs, is truly magical. The ordinary becomes a little extraordinary and life is no longer fragmented. John O'Donohue expressed this best for me when writing about Celtic spirituality: "The physical world was experienced as the shoreline of an invisible world which flowed underneath it and whose music reverberated upwards."[3]

About This Book

Whether you are a beginner or an experienced practitioner, sooner or later when putting together a ritual you may not have enough time, or creative inspiration may remain elusive. This book contains rituals that are "ready to go" for both group and solo practices.

The rituals contained here will take you through a full year of sabbats and esbats. Marking these twenty occasions will help bring you into balance with the rhythms of the natural world. These points in time were important to our ancestors because the sabbats and esbats celebrate the interconnected cycles of the three most important celestial bodies: sun, moon, and earth. Through these celebrations we bring our bodies, minds, and spirits into alignment. These rituals celebrate the cycle of life, death, and rebirth; of the Goddess as maiden, mother, and crone; of God as son, consort, and sage. Through ritual the realms of heaven, the earthly plane, and the underworld are accessible. The Celtic triskele design is a symbol that represents this threefold interconnected flow (Figure 1).

Figure 1—The Celtic triskele

Observing ritual throughout the year keeps us balanced and in tune with nature's cycles (Figure 2). The Chinese yin-yang symbol of balance is a sun chart that was plotted by using an eight-foot pole and recording the length of its shadow through the course of a year.

While this sounds like serious business, ritual is also meant to be joyful. Reverence and joy are not mutually exclusive feelings. The rituals contained in this book are intended to reflect both. They can be easily modified to suit various situations or used simply to brainstorm your own ideas. The group rituals are designed with both Priest and Priestess roles that can be easily changed to accommodate the members and practices of your group. You may also want to change the order in which directions are called to suit your own tradition.

Just as it is important to ground your energy before ending a ritual, it is also essential to prepare yourself beforehand. Appendix E provides a centering exercise that can be read to a group. When working solo, either tape it and play it back or remember it well enough to take yourself through it.

The "Preparation" section of each chapter lists items you will need for the ritual. These are in addition to other objects or decorative material that you would normally use. Most of the items mentioned are fairly standard, however, in situations where something is not readily available—particularly plants such as bittersweet or vines—you may be able to find artificial ones at your local arts and crafts stores. While the real thing might be preferable, remember that intention plays a major role in ritual.

Things we say and do in ritual are symbolic and intended to touch the deeper reaches of our psyches. Within the sacred circle we are outside the bounds of the everyday flow.

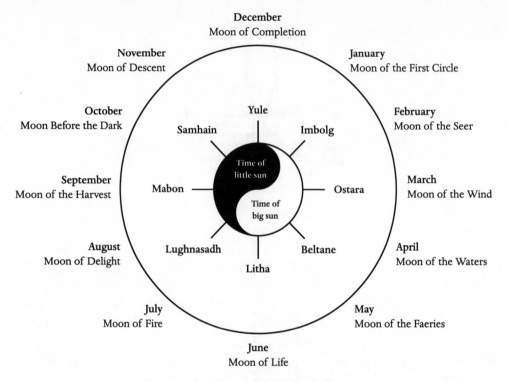

December
Moon of Completion

November
Moon of Descent

January
Moon of the First Circle

October
Moon Before the Dark

Yule

February
Moon of the Seer

Samhain

Imbolg

September
Moon of the Harvest

Time of
little sun

Mabon

Ostara

March
Moon of the Wind

Time of
big sun

August
Moon of Delight

Lughnasadh

Beltane

April
Moon of the Waters

Litha

July
Moon of Fire

May
Moon of the Faeries

June
Moon of Life

Figure 2—The sabbats and full moons

We speak more poetically and our gestures become grander. After all, we are addressing the Divine.

While this book provides ideas, words, and directions for ritual, the most important part must be supplied by you: faith in your beliefs. Without this vital ingredient, ritual is only a performance. Use this book as a framework for your truth. Speak these words and feel them deeply. Make these ideas flow with commitment to your personal spiritual path. Live the magic.

1. Elizabeth Fisher, *Rise Up and Call Her Name* (Boston: Unitarian Universalist Women's Federation, 1994).

2. Ursula K. Le Guin, *A Wizard of Earthsea* (New York: Bantam Spectra, 1984), 44.

3. John O'Donohue, *Eternal Echoes* (New York: HarperCollins Publishers, 1995), 115.

Part I

The Sabbats

The sabbats are a combination of solar and earthly celebrations. The daily cycle of the sun and the seasons of the earth determined the rhythms of activity for our ancestors. They lived close to the land and on an everyday basis observed its subtle changes.

The solar sabbats are called *quarter days* because they separate the year into four parts. The *cross-quarter days* are based on agrarian celebrations, which were extremely important to our ancestors who could not rely on food being trucked in from other places if the harvest was poor. For this reason feasting is an important part of a ritual gathering. While we don't have to worry about harvests and can enjoy almost any kind of food any time of year, if possible, try to have only seasonal foods at sabbat feasts to help you tune into the natural energy level for that particular time of year.

Each sabbat marks a changing point in the year that is accompanied by a shift in energy. If we are open to it, these times of transition can have a physical, mental, and spiritual impact on us. In addition, these turning points carry the mythology and symbolism of the Goddess and God.

The Sabbats: Mother Earth and Father Sun

Following are the basic themes and approximate dates for the celebrations, which can shift by a day or two.

Yule, December 21 (Winter Solstice): Marks the longest night of the year, the return of the light, and the (re)birth of the God.

Imbolg, February 2 (Midwinter): The time of quickening. Halfway between Yule and Ostara, the growing light is definitely noticeable. The baby God is growing and the Goddess is once again a maiden.

Ostara, March 21 (Spring Equinox): This is a time of balance when light and dark, male and female energies are equal. This is the time of courtship between the Maiden and young Lord.

TABLE 1
The Wheel of the Year Marks Solar and Earth Celebrations

GREATER SABBATS (EARTH CROSS-QUARTER DAYS)	LESSER SABBATS (SUN QUARTER DAYS)
Imbolg	Yule
Beltane	Ostara
Lughnasadh	Litha
Samhain	Mabon

Beltane, May 1: Fertility in the "lusty month of May." This marks the sexual union of the Goddess and God. It is a time to feel the vitality of life.

Litha, June 21 (Summer Solstice/Midsummer): The Goddess becomes mother. This is a turning point for the God as his light begins to wane. We celebrate long days and warm weather.

Lughnasadh, August 1 (Lammas): Time of ripeness. Because the Goddess and God provide for us, this is a time to pause and think about the blessings we receive.

Mabon, September 21 (Autumn Equinox): A day of balance. The time of the major harvest and the time to give thanks for abundance. Pagan Thanksgiving. This is the God's last sabbat.

Samhain, October 31: The Goddess is alone as crone. The God has descended to the underworld. We prepare for our journey through the dark of the year.

Even though the Goddess changes throughout the year, she is eternal. She is earth. The God is born and dies each year as the sun passes through its two phases called Big Sun and Little Sun. The waxing and waning of the God also makes him the king and spirit of vegetation. He sprouts from the earth and is the son of the Goddess. He matures and spreads his seed to earth, becoming her consort. At winter he dies, but will be born of the earth again.

The seasonal cycles and all the mythology that has grown up around the Goddess and God provides a comforting continuity. Allow yourself to step outside your everyday world and experience the awe and wonder of this great drama.

Yule

The celebration of Yule is deeply rooted in the cycle of the year and stems from the very ancient practice of honoring the return of the sun after the longest night of the year. A time of transformation, Yule symbolizes the rebirth of the God to the virgin Goddess. The return of the sun/son brings hope and the promise of ongoing life, the coming warmth, and the reawakening of the earth. While the Celts had established Samhain as the beginning of the new year, tenth-century Nordic Pagans moved the new year to Yule to coincide with the solar year.

If the December full moon occurs before the winter solstice, it is traditionally called the Oak Moon. With its roots deep in Mother Earth and its topmost branches high above the ground, the oak was symbolic of living in both the material and spirit worlds. Considered sacred by the Druids, trees figure largely in the Yuletide season. Yule marked the succession from the Holly King (king of the waning year) to the Oak King (king of the waxing year). Holly symbolized death; oak symbolized rebirth.

The use of mistletoe can be traced back to the Druids of Gaul who gathered it from the highest branches of oak trees. Mistletoe is also called "the golden bough" and is considered powerfully magic, especially for fertility. At Yule its white berries are plentiful and symbolize the sacred seed of the God who embodies the spirit of vegetation and the divine spark of life.

At this time of year holly is bright and vital, promising ongoing life. Like holly, evergreen trees were considered sacred because they didn't seem to die each year, and so they represent the eternal aspect of the Goddess. The Great Mother Goddess/Mother

Earth remains constant while the God dies and is reborn each year; endings become beginnings.

With all the sacred trees, holly, and mistletoe brought into the home, it's no accident that Yule is a magical time of year.

Background for This Ritual

Solo practitioners will want to read this just before beginning the ritual. A place has been indicated in the group ritual where this is most appropriate for the Priestess or Priest to read to everyone:

> Putting bright lights on Christmas trees and around the house began with the tradition of lighting candles and fires to honor the return of the sun. The burning Yule log itself represents the new, shining sun. A piece of the Yule log, which is traditionally oak, is kept from one year to the next providing continuity as the old year finishes and the new one begins; death is followed by rebirth. A common component of the Yule ritual, when done outdoors, is to jump a bonfire and make a wish for the coming year. Tonight we combine this basic idea with the spiral, which is associated with the Goddess, winter, and the winter solstice.
>
> The spiral is a fundamental form found in nature. To ancient people, the spiral was a sacred symbol of the Goddess and her transformative powers. Our ancestors knew about, and we are only rediscovering, the vortex of energy in a spiral that allows us to connect with our deepest selves, the web of life, and the Divine.
>
> At the ancient site of Newgrange in Ireland there is a set of three spirals on the back wall of the inner chamber, sixty-five feet from the entrance. On the winter solstice, as well as the day before and the day after, the rising sun illuminates these spirals.
>
> The spiral is also symbolic of winter hibernation. During the cold months we turn inward for a time of reflection. But the same spiral of energy that leads us downward inside ourselves in winter eventually leads us up toward the light in spring.

Themes

- Celebrate the rebirth of the God and the return of light.

- Contemplate the year ahead.

- Make a wish for what you want to bring into your life in the coming year.

Preparation

The items needed for this ritual include the following:

- Five sprigs of holly for group ritual, or four sprigs for solo ritual

- Three strands of gold Christmas tree garland (the longer, the better) for group ritual, or one strand for solo ritual

- Enough tea light candles to place around the perimeter of the three spirals or your entire circle

Make sure the candles are in holders that protect the flame. They will be placed on the floor and you want to protect anyone wearing long clothing from catching fire.

Setup

This ritual does not utilize an altar, although in the group ritual, the space in the middle of the three spirals can function as one.

Use the garland to create three spirals in the center of the floor, making the space within each spiral wide enough to form a path on which to walk. Lay the spirals in such a way that the "entrances" to them are away from each other. Place the sprigs of holly in the center where the three spirals meet. Arrange the candles along the perimeter of each spiral.

For solo ritual, lay out a spiral with one strand of garland (or use two if you would like to make it larger). Place tea lights around the perimeter of the spiral and lay the holly at the entrance.

For both solo and group, light the candles around the spiral(s) just before beginning the ritual.

Group Ritual

Casting the Circle

The Priestess should have a sprig of holly in her hand to begin the ritual.

Priestess   Ancient symbols are all around us in this season. Holly is one of them. At this time of year when most plants have faded, holly is bright and vital, promising ongoing life. The abundance of red berries symbolizes the Goddess's blood—source of all life. May this space be sacred.

The Priestess passes the holly to her left. Each person repeats the phrase:
May this space be sacred.

When the holly returns to the Priestess, she says:
The circle is cast. With the life-giving blood of the Goddess we have created sacred space.

All   Blessed be.

Calling the Quarters

Before evoking a direction, the participants take a sprig of holly from the center of the spirals. When they finish speaking, they place it at the edge of the circle in the respective direction they are calling.

North   Come ye spirits of the north, powers of earth, your bounty sustains us through the winter. Be with us as the silent cavern, a place of renewal. Be with us this night.

All   Be with us this night.

East   Come ye spirits of the east, powers of air, sail on crisp winter wings as you bring the golden dawn. Be with us as a clear night sky. Be with us this night.

All   Be with us this night.

South   Come ye spirits of the south, powers of fire, bring the heat of a flame to warm our hearts. Be with us as a welcoming hearth. Be with us this night.

All   Be with us this night.

West   Come ye spirits of the west, powers of water, you nourish the earth and bathe us in sweet rains. Be with us as a quiet snowfall. Be with us this night.

All   Be with us this night.

Priestess   Great Mother Goddess, provider of all life, Lady of heaven and earth, bring forth your son, transform the light. Be with us this night.

All   Be with us this night.

The Priestess places the sprig of holly used to cast the circle back in the middle of the three spirals.

Background

Share the background information with the group.

Priestess   Tomorrow the sun begins its journey back to us. Tonight we celebrate the rebirth of light.

Priest   Tonight we use the spiral in making our wishes for the new year. Give thought to what you want to bring into your life. When you are ready, follow the path in one of the spirals. When you get to the center, pause and then step over the innermost coil. As you do this, say your wish aloud, and then follow the path out of the spiral.

While some are walking the spirals, the rest of us will do a circle dance around the spirals while chanting:

> With this wish I make,
> And every step I take,
> Bring me to center
> Where my dreams awake.

After everyone has walked a spiral, the Priest and Priestess slow, then end the chant.

Priestess   May our wishes, our intentions voiced here this night, manifest into our physical world. As above, so below. Blessed be.

All   Blessed be.

Priestess   It is time to center ourselves as we move back to the everyday world. Close your eyes. Let your energy spiral down. Feel it touch the earth. Be at peace this winter night. Just as darkness is followed by light, so winter is followed by spring. The Wheel of the Year turns ever onward. When you are ready, open your eyes.

Closing

Priestess   Great Mother who gives birth to the light and gives our world form, we thank you for your presence this night and ask for your blessings as you depart. We bid thee farewell.

All   We bid thee farewell. Blessed be.

Before dismissing their direction, each participant picks up the holly they placed at the edge of the circle. When they finish speaking, they return it to the center of the spirals.

West   Spirits of west, of water that fills the rivers in spring, we thank you for your presence this night. Stay if you will; go if you must. We bid thee farewell.

All   We bid thee farewell. Blessed be.

South   Spirits of south, of fire that provides new beginnings, we thank you for your presence this night. Stay if you will; go if you must. We bid thee farewell.

All   We bid thee farewell. Blessed be.

East   Spirits of east, of air and the precious breath of life, we thank you for your presence this night. Stay if you will; go if you must. We bid thee farewell.

All   We bid thee farewell. Blessed be.

North   Spirits of north, of earth that sustains us, we thank you for your presence this night. Stay if you will; go if you must. We bid thee farewell.

All   We bid thee farewell. Blessed be.

Everyone joins hands.

Priestess   Take time to reflect on the season and on your life. Just as darkness is followed by light, so winter is followed by spring. The Wheel of the Year and of our lives continues to turn. Our circle is open, but unbroken. May love and joy remain in our hearts.

All   "Merry meet, merry part, and merry meet again."[1]

Solo Ritual

Casting the Circle

Pick up the four sprigs of holly and walk around the perimeter of the spiral to define your circle.

Speak

Red and green, holly bright,
Help me cast my circle tonight.
The sun returns, glowing white,
With the child, Lord of Light.

Calling the Quarters

Place a sprig of holly at the edge of your circle in each direction after evoking it.

Come ye spirits of the north, powers of earth, your bounty sustains me through the winter. Be with me as the silent cavern, a place of renewal. Be with me this night.

Come ye spirits of the east, powers of air, sail on crisp winter wings as you bring the golden dawn. Be with me as a clear night sky. Be with me this night.

Come ye spirits of the south, powers of fire, bring the heat of a flame to warm my heart. Be with me as a welcoming hearth. Be with me this night.

Come ye spirits of the west, powers of water, you nourish the earth and bathe me in sweet rains. Be with me as a quiet snowfall. Be with me this night.

Great Mother Goddess, provider of all life, Lady of heaven and earth, bring forth your son, transform the light. Be with me this night.

Tonight I celebrate the return of the sun and the rebirth of light.

Think of what you want to bring into your life. When you are ready, follow the path into the spiral. When you get to the center, pause and then step over the innermost coil. As you do this, say your wish aloud. You may want to pause again or sit in the center of the spiral to contemplate your wish as well as the coming year. When you are ready, follow the path back out of the spiral.

When you emerge from the spiral, begin chanting as you walk around your circle:

> With this wish I make,
> And every step I take,
> Bring me to center
> Where my dreams awake.

When it feels appropriate, slow and then end the chant.

Speak   May my wishes and intentions voiced here this night manifest into the physical world. As above, so below. Blessed be.

Use your usual centering to ground the energy or play back a recorded one.

Closing

Speak   Great Mother who gives birth to the light and gives this world form, thank you for your presence this night. I ask for your blessings as you depart. I bid thee farewell.

As you dismiss each direction, pick up the holly you placed at the edge of your circle and return it to the entrance of the spiral.

Speak   Spirits of east, of water that fills the rivers in spring, thank you for your presence this night. Stay if you will; go if you must. I bid thee farewell.

Spirits of south, of fire that provides new beginnings, thank you for your presence this night. Stay if you will; go if you must. I bid thee farewell.

Spirits of east, of air and the precious breath of life, thank you for your presence this night. Stay if you will; go if you must. I bid thee farewell.

Spirits of north, of earth that sustains me, thank you for your presence this night. Stay if you will; go if you must. I bid thee farewell.

Just as darkness is followed by light, so winter is followed by spring. The Wheel of the Year and of my life continues to turn. My circle is open, but unbroken. May the peace of the Goddess remain in my heart. In faith and unity, blessed be.

---

1. Standard ending; source unknown.

It is at Imbolg/Midwinter when we are halfway between winter solstice and spring equinox that the days become noticeably longer. While winter is not yet over, the promise of spring becomes palatable as receding snow begins to reveal greening grass. Traditionally to celebrate the strengthening sunlight, numerous bonfires and candles were lit. As Christians adopted Pagan practices, Imbolg evolved into Candlemas.

The word *Imbolg* (also spelled *Imbolc*) is derived from an ancient word (possibly Gaelic or Anglo-Saxon) meaning "ewe's milk." In the British Isles this is the time of the lambing season, another promising sign that spring is on the way.

The powerful fire goddess Brigid presides over Imbolg. Her many aspects are called into play at this sabbat. In addition to fire, she is the goddess of holy wells and springs, crossroads (divination), and is a midwife (transformer). As midwife, she helps to "birth" the new year/growing light. She also helps us divine the path we need to follow for self-transformation.

Imbolg is a time of purification and clearing out old things from our lives. As the world is beginning to waken from winter's slumber, it is time to shed the past and move forward with hope.

Background for This Ritual

Solo practitioners will want to read this just before beginning the ritual. A place has been indicated in the group ritual where this is most appropriate for the Priestess or Priest to read to everyone, or it can be read before beginning:

Imbolg is halfway between winter solstice and spring equinox. The time of quickening is at hand. We can see the days grow longer as the infant Lord increases in strength. Imbolg marks the lambing season when ewe's milk flows. This is a time for gentleness and nurturing.

This time of quickening occurs at the crossroads of the year. No one knows what twists and turns lie ahead in the year that has just begun to unfold. As goddess of the crossroads, Brigid will help guide your path. Brigid's cross symbolically unites the four directions/elements (and Ireland's four provinces) with the otherworld/underworld. As the goddess of crossroads, she is said to be able to see where someone has come from as well as where each road might take him or her. Because of this, Imbolg is a time for divination, a time to discern and perhaps choose our path for the year ahead. As you make a Brigid's cross in this ritual, ask her to inspire you as to which path you need to follow in the months ahead.

Themes

- Celebrate the lengthening days.

- Discern a path for the coming months.

- Ask Brigid for guidance.

Preparation

Items needed for this ritual include the following:

- Six green candles

- White altar cloth

- Potted snowdrops and/or crocuses

- A chalice and paper cups for those who might not want to drink from the chalice

- Milk or milk substitute, if necessary

- Oat cakes or oatmeal cookies and a plate to set them on the altar

- Straw or twigs cut to an even length, enough to give a handful to each participant

- White yarn or string

- A deck of tarot cards or a set of runes, consecrated if new

- A candle in a holder that can be set on the floor provided by each person in group ritual, or enough candles to form your circle (minimum of four) for solo ritual

Group Ritual

Each participant holds his or her unlit candle.

Casting the Circle

Priestess   This is Imbolg, Midwinter. The days wax longer as winter loosens its grip on the world. This is the time of hope and renewal. We have come through the dark into the quickening light.

The Priest lights the Priestess's candle. She turns to the person on her left and touches the flame of her candle to his or hers, saying:

Share the light.

Each person repeats this phrase as he or she passes the flame around the circle. When it comes back to the Priestess she says:

The circle is cast. Gloom of winter be gone.

All   Gloom of winter be gone.

Participants place their candles on the floor behind them.

Calling the Quarters

Each person goes to the edge of the circle in his or her respective direction before speaking. The altar candle can be lit before or after speaking. The Priest and Priestess face the altar when evoking the Goddess and God.

North   Spirits of north, powers of earth, beneath the lingering snow life stirs in your bosom awaiting the warmth of spring. We call on your power of quickening. Be with us this night to celebrate the light.

All   Be with us this night to celebrate the light.

East	Spirits of east, powers of air, blow away the dark clouds of winter. Whisper gently to herald the light. We call on your power of awakening. Be with us this night to celebrate the light.
All	Be with us this night to celebrate the light.
South	Spirits of south, powers of fire, rid the world of winter's icy grip. We call on your power to hasten the spring. Be with us this night to celebrate the light.
All	Be with us this night to celebrate the light.
West	Spirits of west, powers of water, bring soothing rains to melt the snow and wash away the staleness of winter. We call on your power to revitalize life. Be with us this night to celebrate the light.
All	Be with us this night to celebrate the light.
Priest	Infant King, son of the Great Mother, you bring the growing light and the hope of spring. Part the darkness with your renewed spirit. Be with us this night to celebrate the light.
All	Be with us this night to celebrate the light.
Priestess	Great Lady Brigid, goddess of healing waters and crossroads, dispel the gloom of winter with your shining love. Be with us this night to celebrate the light.
All	Be with us this night to celebrate the light.

Background

Share the background information here if it was not read before starting the ritual.

Priestess	Bright blessings of Brigid at Midwinter. In this season of the lambs we celebrate nurturing and warmth with milk and oat cakes.

The Priest raises the chalice of milk and plate of oak cakes, then hands the chalice to the Priestess and says:

Sweet oats represent the sweetness of a mother's love.

Priestess   Milk represents the nurturing Goddess.

In unison   May the Goddess give her blessing to this food.

After setting a little of both milk and oat cake aside for the Goddess, the Priest goes to the north side of the circle. Placing a piece of oak cake in each participant's mouth, he says:
      May Brigid's love sweeten your life.

The Priestess holds the chalice as each participant takes a sip of the milk. She says:
      May Brigid's love nurture your path.

When they have completed a circuit of the circle, the Priest and Priestess minister the rite to each other.

Priestess   We stand at the crossroads of the year where Brigid will meet us. If we ask, she will guide us.

The Priest takes the basket of straw/twigs and gives an even-numbered amount to each participant along with a length of white yarn.

Priest   To make Brigid's cross, take half of the straws in each hand. Lay one set perpendicular to the other, creating an equal-armed cross. Wrap the yarn over and under at the center to secure them. While you work, let your mind roam freely and think of yourself approaching a crossroads. When you arrive, Brigid is standing in the middle. She points to one of the roads.

When you finish making your cross, close your eyes and hold it between your hands. Meditate on the path Brigid pointed out for you. Let this path inspire you; let it bring you to a place of beauty. Let these thoughts and images flow into the cross you hold.

The Priest or other designated participant may drum a steady rhythm.

Priest   As you hold the vision of the crossroads in your mind, it may feel appropriate to stand or move around the circle.

When everyone has finished their cross and had a chance to meditate or move around the circle, bring the drumming to stillness.

Priestess	Now that we have asked the Goddess to set us on our paths, it is time to bring the energy down and begin to move back to our everyday level of awareness.

Close your eyes and become aware of the energy slowly unwinding through you. Feel it move down through your body. Become aware of your feet on the floor and the energy running from you through the floor to Mother Earth.

When you feel centered and grounded, you can stop sending energy. When you are ready, open your eyes.

Closing

Each participant extinguishes the candle they lit during the evocation.

Priestess	Great Lady, Brigid, we thank you for your guidance this night and for joining us in our circle. Stay if you will; go if you must. We bid you farewell. Blessed be.
All	We bid you farewell. Blessed be.
Priest	Young Son, bringer of light, may you grow strong and bright as the year progresses. Stay if you will; go if you must. We bid you farewell. Blessed be.
All	We bid you farewell. Blessed be.
West	Spirits of west, powers of water, we thank you for the warming rains and your presence this night. Stay if you will; go if you must. We bid you farewell. Blessed be.
All	We bid you farewell. Blessed be.
South	Spirits of south, powers of fire, we thank you for piercing the darkness and for your presence this night. Stay if you will; go if you must. We bid you farewell. Blessed be.
All	We bid you farewell. Blessed be.

East   Spirits of east, powers of air, we thank you for a breath of spring and for your presence this night. Stay if you will; go if you must. We bid you farewell. Blessed be.

All   We bid you farewell. Blessed be.

North   Spirits of north, powers of earth, we thank you for safekeeping life in your welcoming body and for your presence this night. Stay if you will; go if you must. We bid you farewell. Blessed be.

All   We bid you farewell. Blessed be.

Priestess   We extinguish the light of our circle, but its spark will remain in our hearts.

Participants pick up the candles that formed the circle and put out the flames.

Priestess   Our circle is open but unbroken. May the growing light of the returning Lord remain kindled in our hearts.

All   Merry meet, merry part, and merry meet again.

Solo Ritual

Casting the Circle

Walk around and place candles on the floor to mark your circle as you say:

> As the sun grows bright,
> Welcome, Lord of Light.
> As the days wax long,
> Gloom of winter be gone.

Calling the Quarters

Light a green candle on the altar as you evoke each direction or deity.

Speak   Spirits of north, powers of earth, beneath the lingering snow life stirs in your bosom awaiting the warmth of spring. I call on your power of quickening. Be with me this night to celebrate the light.

Spirits of east, powers of air, blow away the dark clouds of winter. Whisper gently to herald the light. I call on your power of awakening. Be with me this night to celebrate the light.

Spirits of south, powers of fire, rid the world of winter's icy grip. I call on your power to hasten the spring. Be with me this night to celebrate the light.

Spirits of west, powers of water, bring soothing rains to melt the snow and wash away the staleness of winter. I call on your power to revitalize life. Be with me this night to celebrate the light.

Infant King, son of the Great Mother, you bring the growing light and the hope of spring. Part the darkness with your renewed spirit. Be with me this night to celebrate the light.

Great Lady Brigid, goddess of healing waters and crossroads, dispel the gloom of winter with your shining love. Be with me this night to celebrate the light.

Raise the chalice of milk and plate of oak cakes in an offertory gesture above your altar, then say:

Tonight I celebrate this quickening time with milk and oat cakes. Sweet oats represent the sweetness of a mother's love. Milk represents the nurturing Goddess. I call on you, sweet Mother, to bless this food.

Before taking a bite of oak cake, say:

May Brigid's love sweeten my life.

Before taking a sip of milk, say:

May Brigid's love nurture my path.

Take half of the straw or twigs in each hand. Lay one set perpendicular to the other, creating an equal-armed cross. Wrap the yarn over and under at the center to secure them. As you work, chant:

As spell of winter soon will break,
This cross by candlelight I make.
With twists and turns, yarn drawn tight,
Brigid guide me through the night.

When you finish, close your eyes and hold the cross between your hands. Meditate on the path you feel drawn to follow this year. Ask Brigid for guidance. When you feel ready to move back to the everyday world, ground your energy.

Closing

Extinguish each candle on the altar as you speak.

Speak   Great Lady, Brigid, thank you for your guidance this night and for joining me in my circle. Stay if you will; go if you must. Farewell and blessed be.

Young Son, bringer of light, may you grow strong and bright as the year progresses. Stay if you will; go if you must. Farewell and blessed be.

Spirits of west, powers of water, thank you for the warming rains and your presence this night. Stay if you will; go if you must. Farewell and blessed be.

Spirits of south, powers of fire, thank you for piercing the darkness and for your presence this night. Stay if you will; go if you must. Farewell and blessed be.

Spirits of east, powers of air, thank you for a breath of spring and for your presence this night. Stay if you will; go if you must. Farewell and blessed be.

Spirits of north, powers of earth, thank you for safekeeping life in your welcoming body and for your presence this night. Stay if you will; go if you must. Farewell and blessed be.

As you put out the candles that formed your circle, say:

I extinguish the light of this circle, but its spark will remain in my heart. My circle is open but unbroken. May the growing light of the returning Lord remain kindled in my heart. Blessed be.

Ostara

Ostara is the Latin name for the Saxon spring goddess, Eostre. Her counterpart in ancient Greece was Eos, also called Aurora. The vernal equinox is a time of balance when day and night are equal. It is a day to celebrate both the earth and sun. Our ancestors included the symbolic sexual union of Goddess and God in their rituals and honored the balance of all things: female and male, spiritual and physical. In Celtic Cornwall and Wales, Ostara was called Lady Day and celebrated the return of the Goddess after her winter hibernation.

In the maiden-mother-crone cycle of the Goddess and seasons, the maiden phase is now unfolding as the earth renews herself. Signs of reawakening life can be seen everywhere as snowdrops and crocuses emerge and trees come into bud. This season brings freshness into our lives and new perspectives as we shed heavy winter clothes and feel the warmth of the sun on our bodies.

One of the most well-known stories of the Maiden Goddess is that of Demeter and her daughter Persephone (also called Kore). Persephone felt that it was her calling to go to the underworld to comfort and guide the spirits of the dead to their rest. Even though Demeter knew her daughter would return, she put her life on hold and waited. During this time, grain and other plants didn't grow and the weather was cold. When Persephone returned bringing warmth and love for her mother, the entire earth came alive again. Later (ancient Greek) versions of this story added violence with Persephone being kidnapped to the underworld by Hades and Zeus bargaining with Demeter to bring the plants back to life. Happily, this gentler version is gaining popularity.

Eggs, which symbolized sacred life to our ancestors, were decorated to honor the Goddess and given as gifts. In the Middle Ages decorated eggs were used as Easter tithes to parish priests. Present-day Wiccans and Pagans decorate eggs with symbols such as circles and spirals, the sun, and the Tree of Life.

Background for This Ritual

This ritual has been written for daytime to enjoy the warmth, light, and greening earth. Solo practitioners will want to read this just before beginning the ritual. A place has been indicated in the group ritual where this is most appropriate for the Priestess or Priest to read to everyone, or it can be read before beginning:

> Ostara celebrates both the sun and the earth. It is a day to celebrate the balance of all things: female and male, the spiritual and the physical. The spiral you walked at winter solstice took you down inside yourself. Now is the time to follow that spiral of energy up into the light.
>
> As Persephone reemerges from the underworld, animals return from their winter hibernation. One such creature is the snake, an ancient symbol of the Great Mother Goddess. Snakes dwell in both worlds: ours and the underworld. Because they live underground, they carry the power of Mother Earth. Into the time of ancient Greece the snake was a symbol of earthly powers especially for healing. Even today it is included in the symbol of the medical profession.

Themes

- Seek balance and growth.
- Plant seeds of intention.
- Summon earth energy to manifest intention.

Preparation

Items needed for this ritual include the following:

- Four green altar candles for the directions
- Two lavender or purple altar candles for the Goddess and God

- At least one cut flower for each participant in group ritual, or enough flowers to mark your circle (minimum of four) for solo ritual

- Flower seeds—daisies, if possible, as this flower is associated with spring, light, and the sun

- A small flowerpot or small paper cup filled with potting soil for each participant, and, if you like, decorated with Pagan symbols such as a pentagram, spiral, or a circle with a dot in the center

- One or two plastic but realistic-looking snakes

FOR SOLO RITUAL

In addition to the above, the following will also be needed:

- One or two long scarves

- Taped music or drumming with which to dance (optional)

- Taped grounding/centering (optional)

Group Ritual

Priestess   This is the time of spring's return, the seed time, a joyful time when life bursts from the womb of earth breaking the shackles of winter. The equinox is a time of balance when night and day, light and dark are equal.

Now, the young Prince of Light born at winter solstice meets Persephone, the Dark Maiden who returns from her time in the underworld. As they dance, flowers appear and warm sunlight greens the earth.

May our hearts open with the return of spring to find renewal and harmony.

Casting the Circle

The Priestess passes a flower to the person on her left saying:
        We welcome the return of spring.

Each participant repeats the phrase as he or she passes the flower. When it arrives back to the Priestess, she says:

With this gift from the Goddess we have created sacred space where the realms flow together.

Calling the Quarters

After each direction and deity is called, the participant lights a candle on the altar.

North   Come ye spirits of the north, powers of earth, hold us rooted by tree and flower. Bring us the beauty of your lush green meadows. Be with us this day.

All   Be with us this day.

East   Come ye spirits of the east, powers of air, sail on golden wings of dawn. Blow away the staleness of winter. Be with us this day.

All   Be with us this day.

South   Come ye spirits of the south, powers of fire, bring the heat of noon to warm our days. Coax the seeds from the womb of the earth. Be with us this day.

All   Be with us this day.

West   Come ye spirits of the west, powers of water, let our souls flow with the beauty of your tides. Bless the land with dew-filled mornings. Be with us this day.

All   Be with us this day.

Priest   Prince of Light, Lord of spring, you wax to the fullness of youth and bless the world with your bright spirit. Join us in this sacred circle. Be with us this day.

All   Be with us this day.

Priestess   Great Mother who gives our world form, as your web of life renews the earth, light that spark within us to awaken our souls. Join us in this sacred circle. Be with us this day.

All   Be with us this day.

Background

Share the background information here if it was not read before starting the ritual.

The Priestess gives each participant a small flowerpot (or paper cup) filled with soil. The Priest gives each person several flower seeds.

Priestess   Hold the seeds in the palm of one hand, then cup your other hand over it. Close your eyes. At winter solstice we made wishes and set forth intentions for the new year. Now is the time to start bringing those wishes and intentions into the physical world.

Fix that wish or intention in your mind. Let the energy and vision flow from you into the seeds. Visualize your wish coming to fruition. Once you have clearly seen what you want to achieve or receive, open your eyes and then place the seeds into the cup and cover them lightly with soil. When you take it home, put it in a place where you will see it frequently and be reminded of your intention.

Priest   Today we use the symbol of the snake and summon the earthly powers of the Goddess. We call forth this power to energize the seeds we have planted by doing a snake dance.

Begin as a circle with everyone holding hands except for the person who will lead the dance. If moving deosil, he or she will not hold the hand of the person on his or her left. Begin by spiraling toward the center of the circle, then curve away so that passing dancers are facing each other. You can weave in and out between other dancers or have two people create a bridge with their arms under which others will pass. The dance can move fast or slow or alternate speeds. Several members may choose to drum as others dance.

Priestess   As we dance, we call forth the power of the Mother Goddess with chant:

Gaia rising, Gaia rising;
Mother of love, mother of life.

Once everyone picks up the chant the Priest and Priestess may choose to sing the counterchant:

Gaia, Gaia, mother of all.
Gaia, Gaia, we heed your call.

After the dancing and chanting reaches its peak, the Priest gradually slows the pace, then brings it to an end.

Priestess	It is time to end our circle. Close your eyes. Release the energy. Send it out to the seeds we have planted. And now, become aware of your feet on the floor. You may also want to place your hands on the floor to send the excess energy to earth. Touch your energy to Mother Earth. Feel your energy spiral down through you to her. When you feel balanced and grounded, stop sending energy. And when you are ready, open your eyes.

Closing

Each participant, in turn, puts out the candle he or she lit at the beginning of the ritual.

Priestess	Great Mother, we ask that your blessings remain in our hearts and that we live in harmony with all that dwell on this earth. We thank you for your presence this day. Stay if you will; go if you must. We bid you farewell.
All	We bid you farewell.
Priest	Lord of the spring and budding new life, we welcome the growth and beauty that you bestow upon the greening land. We thank you for your presence this day. Stay if you will; go if you must. We bid you farewell.
All	We bid you farewell.
West	Spirits of the west, of waters that nourish the land, we thank you for your presence this day. Stay if you will; go if you must. We bid you farewell.
All	We bid you farewell.
South	Spirits of the south, of fire that provides new beginnings, we thank you for your presence this day. Stay if you will; go if you must. We bid you farewell.
All	We bid you farewell.
East	Spirits of the east, of air and precious breath, we thank you for your presence this day. Stay if you will; go if you must. We bid you farewell.
All	We bid you farewell.

North	Spirits of the north, of earth that brings forth new life, we thank you for your presence this day. Stay if you will; go if you must. We bid you farewell.
All	We bid you farewell.

Everyone joins hands around the circle.

Priestess

As all good things must sometimes end,
Go forth with the love the Goddess sends.
For if your heart is always true,
This circle will come back to you.

All	Merry meet, merry part, and merry meet again. Blessed be.

Solo Ritual

Casting the Circle

Lay the flowers on the floor as you cast your circle and say:

Equal is the light and dark,
With these gifts my circle I mark.
As warm sunlight greens the earth,
The Maiden and Lord dance with mirth.

Calling the Quarters

After calling each direction and deity, light a candle on the altar.

Speak	Come ye spirits of the north, powers of earth, hold me rooted by tree and flower. Bring the beauty of your lush green meadows. Be with me this day.
	Come ye spirits of the east, powers of air, sail on golden wings of dawn. Blow away the staleness of winter. Be with me this day.
	Come ye spirits of the south, powers of fire, bring the heat of noon to warm my days. Coax the seeds from the womb of the earth. Be with me this day.

Come ye spirits of the west, powers of water, let my soul flow with the beauty of your tides. Bless the land with dew-filled mornings. Be with me this day.

Prince of Light, Lord of spring, you wax to the fullness of youth and bless the world with your bright spirit. Join me in this sacred circle. Be with me this day.

Great Mother who gives the world form, as your web of life renews the earth, light that spark within me to awaken my soul. Join me in this sacred circle. Be with me this day.

Stand in front of the altar. Hold a few of the flower seeds in the palm of one hand, then cup your other hand over it. Close your eyes, and recall that at winter solstice you made a wish and set forth an intention for the new year. Now is the time to start bringing them into the physical world.

Fix that wish or intention in your mind. Let the energy and vision flow from you into the seeds. Visualize your wish coming to fruition. Once you have clearly seen what you want to achieve or receive, open your eyes and then place the seeds into the cup and cover them lightly with soil. After your ritual, put it in a place where you will see it frequently and be reminded of your intention.

Call forth the power of the snake to energize the seeds you have planted by dancing around your circle. Unfurl the scarves and shake them to create an undulating motion to simulate the movement of a snake. If you are using taped music or drumming, begin it now.

As you dance, call forth the power of the Mother Goddess with a chant:

Gaia rising, Gaia rising;
Mother of love, mother of life.

You may want to alternate this with the counterchant:

Gaia, Gaia, mother of all.
Gaia, Gaia, we heed your call.

When your energy has been released, bring your dancing and chanting (and taped music, if used) to a close. Use your usual method for grounding.

Closing

Extinguish the altar candles in the reverse order that they were lit.

Speak   Great Mother, I ask that your blessings remain in my heart and that I live in harmony with all that dwell on this earth. Thank you for your presence this day. Stay if you will; go if you must. I bid you farewell.

Lord of the spring and budding new life, I welcome the growth and beauty that you bestow upon the greening land. Thank you for your presence this day. Stay if you will; go if you must. I bid you farewell.

Spirits of the west, of waters that nourish the land, thank you for your presence this day. Stay if you will; go if you must. I bid you farewell.

Spirits of the south, of fire that provides new beginnings, thank you for your presence this day. Stay if you will; go if you must. I bid you farewell.

Spirits of the east, of air and precious breath, thank you for your presence this day. Stay if you will; go if you must. I bid you farewell.

Spirits of the north, of earth that brings forth new life, thank you for your presence this day. Stay if you will; go if you must. I bid you farewell.

Raise your arms as you stand facing your altar, and say:

> As all good things must sometimes end,
> Go forth with the love the Goddess sends.
> For if your heart is always true,
> The circle will come back to you.

Beltane

Beltane falls directly opposite Samhain on the Wheel of the Year. Both sabbats mark points in time when the veil between the worlds is particularly thin.

The traditional bonfire on May Eve was started from a bundle of wood that came from nine types of trees. The bundle was wrapped with ribbons and adorned with flowers. A small smoldering piece of the fire was carried to each person's home to ensure summer blessings.

The most widespread and enduring of Beltane rituals is the dance around the maypole on May 1. The tree for the pole was usually a type of fir with the top branches intact. In some parts of Europe the branches were replaced by a Christian cross. Just the mention of the word *maypole* conjures up images of costumed dancers weaving a spiral dance while winding red and white ribbons down the pole, raising energy for (pro)creation. Beltane is a celebration of the union of the Goddess and God, fertility, new life, and resurrection. At this time of year the Goddess's mother aspect is in youthful bloom. The phallic symbol of the pole represents the Green Man.

May is strongly associated with other worlds. Just as the veil between the worlds is thin at Samhain, so it is at Beltane and the unseen can be seen. The faery folk are particularly active during this month. Watch for faery rings of toadstools or flowers, and leave an offering in the woods to make friends with them.

May is also a good time to leave offerings at wells and springs. During this time the healing powers of water from sacred wells is amplified. The water of life is especially important at this time of year when crops are just beginning to grow. In ancient Rome, coins and other offerings were left at wells and pools, and the tradition continues unabated year round at the Trevi fountain, which originally honored the Roman goddess Trivia.

Background for This Ritual

Solo practitioners will want to read this just before beginning the ritual. A place has been indicated in the group ritual where this is most appropriate for the Priestess or Priest to read to everyone, or it can be read before beginning:

> Beltane is a celebration of the union of the Goddess and God, a celebration of fertility and new life. The maypole, a phallic symbol representing the king and spirit of vegetation, is planted into Mother Earth to symbolize union and balance.
>
> May is a month of special magic. Looking at the Wheel of the Year, you see that Beltane is opposite Samhain. Just as Samhain is associated with other worlds, so it is Beltane when the unseen can be seen. It was on May Eve that the Tuatha de Danann (tribe of the goddess Danu) arrived in Ireland. They later took refuge in the hollow hills and became known as the people of the hills and the sídhe. We've all heard of them—we know them as the faeries. They are masters of enchantment and in May their magic is strongest.
>
> More than any other time of year, the waters of May are particularly potent, especially for healing. Even today, the Chalice Well at Glastonbury, England, the Cullonden Well in Scotland, and many other places all over Europe are sites of pilgrimage for spiritual and healing purposes.
>
> Brigid, known in Ireland as goddess of fire and inspiration, is honored on February 2. She is also important at Beltane because she presides over water, holy wells, and healing. To some, she is also known as the Queen of the Faeries.

Themes

- Celebrate of the union of the Goddess and God.
- Call on the power of faeries for enchantment.
- Enact a holy well offering.

Preparation

Items for this ritual include the following:

- Two white candles for deities

- Four candles for the directions in pastel shades or colors of bright flowers

- Chalice or small paper cups for participants who do not want to drink from the chalice

- Athame

- Sweet juice such as peach nectar

- Shelled sunflower seeds on a plate suitable for the altar

- Cauldron filled with water

- Enough pennies for all participants set on a tray or plate next to the cauldron

- Drums or other percussion instruments to accompany chanting (optional)

Group Ritual

Priestess   This is Beltane, the sweet time of year when desire and delight awaken in our bodies and souls.

Priest   The Lord of the Waxing Year and the Maiden of Spring meet in the greening meadows and rejoice in the warm sunlight.

Priestess   We meet in this time of flowering to dance the sweet dance of life.

Casting the Circle

Priestess   We cast our circle by naming ourselves. I am _____.

After each person says his or her name, she continues:

With this circle we have passed through the gates of time. We are between the worlds in sacred space.

Calling the Quarters

Each participant walks to the edge of the circle in his or her respective direction, then lights a candle on the altar after speaking. The Priest and Priestess stand in front of the altar to evoke deity.

North	We look to the north, to Falias. Dark Mother, rich black soil, your fertile body nurtures the seeds of life. We call on your powers of creation. Be with us.
All	Be with us, Dark Mother.
East	We look to the east, to Gorias. Star Sailor, holy breath, your clear blue skies smile on us and carry the lusty scent of life. Be with us.
All	Be with us, Star Sailor.
South	We look to the south, to Finias. Blue Flame, light of the earth, your warmth makes us dance with delight at the life that flows through our bodies. Be with us.
All	Be with us, Blue Flame.
West	We look to the west, to Murias. Rainmaker, sacred dew, your gentle rains pour forth in life-giving wonder. Be with us.
All	Be with us, Rainmaker.
Priest	Prince Sun, lord of the dance, winter-born king, bring forth your sacred seed of life. Be with us.
All	Be with us, Lord of Life.
Priestess	Sweet Maiden, lady of the lake, queen of heaven and earth, receive the sacred seed of life. Be with us.
All	Be with us, Lady of All.
Priestess	At this time of year the Goddess, in her maiden aspect, comes of age as the earth is blossoming and fertile. Tonight we celebrate the union of the Goddess and God.

At the altar, the Priestess takes up the chalice, and the Priest the athame. Slowly, he lowers the athame into the raised chalice to symbolize the Great Rite.

In unison   This is Beltane, a time to celebrate life, a time to create life, the Lord and Lady join as one. The Lord and Lady share the dance of life. The Lord and Lady share the kiss of life.

The Priest and Priestess end with a kiss. The chalice is filled with a sweet juice. The Priest takes the plate of sunflower seeds. Beginning at the north point of the circle the Priest places a few seeds in each participant's mouth and the Priestess gives each a sip from the chalice, saying:

Priest   Share the seed of life.

Priestess   Share the nectar of life.

After each participant has received each, the Priest and Priestess minister to each other.

Background

Share the background information here if it was not read before starting the ritual.

Priest   Tonight, our cauldron is filled with water to represent a holy well. The cauldron is a symbol of the womb of the Goddess and place of transformation. Tonight, as we dance and celebrate life, we call on the power of faery to add enchantment to our personal intentions.

As we begin dancing, fix your intention in your mind. You may be thinking of love, of a special someone you want to attract. You may call on Brigid for healing, or you may simply want to give thanks for the joy of living. When you are ready, break away from the dance, take a coin from the tray beside the cauldron, then walk around the altar three times whispering your intention. When you arrive back at the cauldron, drop the coin into the water, then rejoin the dance.

Priestess   As we dance we will chant:

> Holy well, enchanted land,
> Take this coin from my hand.
> With my wish now set free,
> Make it real, so mote it be.

Some participants may choose to drum instead of dance (or in addition to dancing). When all of the participants have thrown a coin into the cauldron and the dancing/chanting has reached its peak, the Priest and Priestess bring the energy down.

Priestess   May our joy, celebration, and intentions be carried out into the world. As above, so below.

All   As above, so below.

Priest   It is time to move back to our everyday world. Close your eyes, let your breath settle into a comfortable rhythm. Let go of the momentum of dancing and feel your energy spiral down. Let it bring relaxation down through your body. Feel the heat of your body flow down through you as the energy unwinds. Let it flow down, down to your feet and then continue through the floor. Let your energy continue below this building. Touch your energy to Mother Earth.

As your energy and heat flows downward, you may feel a heaviness through your body as you come back into everyday awareness. Take time to reflect on the celebration tonight. Reflect on the power of enchantment. Reflect on the power of your life. When you are ready, open your eyes.

Closing
Each participant, in turn, puts out the candle he or she lit at the beginning of the ritual.

Priestess   Sweet Maiden of May, we thank you for your blessings and presence this night. Stay if you will; go if you must. We bid you farewell.

All   We bid you farewell, Sweet Maiden of May.

Priest   Lord of Life, we thank you for your blessings and presence this night. Stay if you will; go if you must. We bid you farewell.

All   We bid you farewell, Lord of Life.

West   Rainmaker, we thank you for your blessings and presence this night. Stay if you will; return to Murias if you must. We bid you farewell.

All   We bid you farewell, Rainmaker.

South	Blue Flame, we thank you for your blessings and presence this night. Stay if you will; return to Finias if you must. We bid you farewell.
All	We bid you farewell, Blue Flame.
East	Star Sailor, we thank you for your blessings and presence this night. Stay if you will; return to Gorias if you must. We bid you farewell.
All	We bid you farewell, Star Sailor.
North	Dark Mother, we thank you for your blessings and presence this night. Stay if you will; return to Falias if you must. We bid you farewell.
All	We bid you farewell, Dark Mother.

Everyone joins hands around the circle.

Priestess	By the four great cities of the faery realm, by the four great powers from beyond, our circle is open, but unbroken. May the peace of Danu remain in our hearts.
All	Merry meet, merry part, and merry meet again. Blessed be.

Solo Ritual

Casting the Circle

With athame raised high in one hand, walk the perimeter of your circle, saying:

> Star light, star bright,
> I call the faeries forth tonight,
> Come and celebrate with me,
> Dance and sing, so mote it be.

Calling the Quarters

Face each direction as you call it, and then light a candle. Face the altar for the Goddess and God.

Speak	I look to the north, to Falias. Dark Mother, rich black soil, your fertile body nurtures the seeds of life. I call on your powers of creation. Be with me.

I look to the east, to Gorias. Star Sailor, holy breath, your clear blue skies smile on me and carry the lusty scent of life. Be with me.

I look to the south, to Finias. Blue Flame, light of the earth, your warmth makes me dance with delight at the life that flows through my body. Be with me.

I look to the west, to Murias. Rainmaker, sacred dew, your gentle rains pour forth in life-giving wonder. Be with me.

Prince Sun, lord of the dance, winter-born king, bring forth your sacred seed of life. Be with me.

Sweet Maiden, lady of the lake, queen of heaven and earth, receive the sacred seed of life. Be with me.

At the altar, take the chalice in one hand and the athame in the other. Slowly, lower the athame into the raised chalice to symbolize the Great Rite while saying:

This is Beltane, a time to celebrate life, a time to create life, the Lord and Lady join as one. The Lord and Lady share the dance of life. The Lord and Lady share the kiss of life.

Kiss the rim of the chalice. Before eating a few sunflower seeds and taking a sip from the chalice, say the following, respectively:

I partake of the seed of life.

I partake of the nectar of life.

Tonight, the cauldron is filled with water to represent a holy well. The cauldron is a symbol of the womb of the Goddess and place of transformation. Tonight, dance and celebrate life, and call on the power of faery to add enchantment to your personal intentions.

Fix an intention in your mind. It might be about love and someone you want to attract. You may call on Brigid for healing, or you may simply want to give thanks for the joy of living. When you are ready, take a coin from the tray beside the cauldron, then walk around the altar three times, whispering your intention. When you arrive back at the cauldron, drop the coin into the water, then dance and chant:

Holy well, enchanted land,

Take this coin from my hand.

> With my wish now set free,
> Make it real, so mote it be.

When it feels appropriate, slow your dancing and say:

> May my joy, celebration, and intention be carried out into the world. As above, so below.

Use your usual method for grounding energy.

Closing

Extinguish the candles in reverse order.

Speak   Sweet Maiden of May, thank you for your blessings and presence this night. Stay if you will; go if you must. I bid you farewell.

Lord of Life, thank you for your blessings and presence this night. Stay if you will; go if you must. I bid you farewell.

Rainmaker, thank you for your blessings and presence this night. Stay if you will; return to Murias if you must. I bid you farewell.

Blue Flame, thank you for your blessings and presence this night. Stay if you will; return to Finias if you must. I bid you farewell.

Star Sailor, thank you for your blessings and presence this night. Stay if you will; return to Gorias if you must. I bid you farewell.

Dark Mother, thank you for your blessings and presence this night. Stay if you will; return to Falias if you must. I bid you farewell.

Standing in front of the altar, say:

> By the four great cities of the faery realm, by the four powers from beyond, my circle is open, but unbroken. May the peace of Danu remain in my heart. In faith and unity, blessed be.

Litha

Summer solstice falls midway between the two equinoxes. The ancient Celtic year consisted of two primary seasons with summer (big sun) beginning at Beltane and winter (little sun) beginning at Samhain. Summer solstice is also referred to as Litha from the Anglo-Saxon phrase *Aerra Litha,* which meant "before midsummer." Themes for this passage of the year are fertility and fire.

In the Dianic tradition, this is a celebration of the Goddess's power of fire. Hestia, Vesta, Pele, Artemis, and Brigid are specifically honored. The Great Goddess is in her full mother aspect. She is the full moon of summer. It is a time of year when everything is ripening. This aspect is synonymous with adulthood and knowledge, as well as developing the body, mind, and spirit in balance. Litha celebrates the Sun King and Queen of Summer. For the Sun King (known as Lugh and Beli Mawr to the Celts) this is more or less a wake because as the Wheel of the Year makes this turn, he begins his decline into darkness.

Like many celebrations throughout the year, bonfires were an important part of the revelry. In the farming communities of Europe, ashes from the solstice bonfire were sprinkled over the fields to promote fertility of the land. It was also a time when our ancestors would seek the Goddess's blessing and protection for the animals on which their livelihoods depended.

As late as the eighteenth century in England, bonfires would be lit on all the hilltops around the countryside. Like other sabbats, Litha is a time for divination, and the embers from the bonfire are used to tell fortunes. Oak is generally used to create a long-burning fire. Oak is significant at this time of year because in the Celtic tree calendar, June (or most of it) is the month of oak. Throughout the year Druids worshipped in sacred oak groves.

Stonehenge is the most famous of monuments that mark the sun's course, but there are many others, some of which are a mix of Pagan and Christian tradition. For example, on the flagstone floor of Chartres Cathedral in France, the midday summer solstice sun casts a circle of light on a diamond-shaped stone.

The herb St. John's wort is in full bloom in June; a sprig of it was placed over the doorways of houses, as well as tossed onto the solstice bonfire to guard against faery mischief. In medieval England, garlands of St. John's wort were woven with marigolds and ivy. These were placed around the necks of farm animals. St. John's wort has been used medicinally for more than two thousand years, and is still a favorite of many herbalists for a range of ailments.

Background for This Ritual

Solo practitioners will want to read this just before beginning the ritual. This background is in two parts, and separate places have been indicated in the group ritual where it is most appropriate for the Priestess or Priest to share with everyone:

Part I: This is the time to rededicate yourself to your spiritual path and to ask for Lugh's blessings. In this ritual marigolds are used to pay homage to the Lord. This flower has been associated with the sun since ancient times and abounds in stories of Apollo, the Greek sun god. Marigolds were believed to have magical properties, and that to look at them or smell their fragrance would remove sorrow and burdens.

Part II: The ancient people of Europe left their legacy in stone all over the continent, the Mediterranean area, and the British Isles in the form of standing stone circles, alignments, and dolmens (chambers formed of standing stones). It has been known for a long time that these places mark the rising and setting of the sun at the winter and summer solstices. They also mark lunar cycles, eclipses, and other astrological events.

It is worth noting that these sites were observatories as well as places of ritual. Science and spirituality were not separate compartments of reasoning and belief. Observing and honoring the natural world were integrated practices.

Stonehenge in England and Newgrange in Ireland are the most well-known sites, but the Brittany coast of France has the greatest number of standing stones. At Carnac in Brittany, within a five-mile area there are three thousand standing stones. Some are in circles, some are alone, but most are in rows that run for several kilometers. For many centuries people danced and celebrated among the stones. Imagine yourself there in Carnac, and feel the energy of the sacred stones.

Themes

- Acknowledge the God as he begins his slow descent after the sun reaches its zenith.

- Honor the God and ask for his blessings.

- Celebrate the warm days of summer.

Preparation

Items for this ritual include the following:

- Six candles for the altar

- A basket of flowers with one cut flower (of any type) for each participant in group ritual, or enough cut flowers to lay out a circle for solo ritual

- A basket of marigolds with one marigold for each participant

- Drums, rattles, and other percussion instruments, or similar taped music, such as Loreena McKennitt's "Huron 'Beltane' Fire Dance"[1]

Also, if doing ritual out of doors, find six to eight large rocks and set them in two rows with enough room for people to walk between to simulate the rows of standing stones at Carnac. If no large stones are available you may want to arrange a pile of smaller stones. If you are doing ritual indoors, use multiple baskets of flowers or potted plants. Be imaginative.

Group Ritual

Priestess   This is the longest day of the year, and we gather to celebrate light and warmth. Summer is new and comes to us softly. Today we call on the

Lord and Lady to awaken the sacred flame within our souls to burn brightly through the days ahead.

Casting the Circle

Priestess   We cast our circle by taking a flower from the basket.

The Priestess removes a flower, and then passes the basket to her left, saying:
With the beauty of summer we create our circle.

Each participant repeats the phrase as he or she takes a flower. When everybody has one, the flowers are placed on the ground in a circle large enough to encompass the "standing stones." The Priestess says:
With this fragrant circle we create sacred space where the seen and unseen join in celebration.

Calling the Quarters

Each person making an evocation goes to the edge of the circle in his or her respective direction. (When doing ritual outdoors, it sometimes works better for the participant to stand in the opposite direction and speak from behind the others in order to be heard.) After speaking, they light a candle on the altar. The Priest and Priestess stand at the altar to do their evocations.

North   We look to the north and call on the powers of earth to join us in our circle. Your body sends forth the blooms of early summer with rich sensuous colors. Be with us as a bright red flower.

All   Be with us this day.

East   We look to the east and call on the powers of air to join us in our circle. Caress us with your warm breezes that sweeten our lives with soft-scented flowers and plants. Be with us as the fragrant linden.

All   Be with us this day.

South   We look to the south and call on the powers of fire to join us in our circle. Your growing heat transforms the world into a lush garden. Kiss us gently with your warmth.

All   Be with us this day.

West	We look to the west and the powers of water. Your gentle rains banish thirst and wash us clean. Touch us with dew-filled mornings.
All	Be with us this day.
Priest	Sun King, lord of summer, we welcome you at your zenith, your last full shining. Tomorrow you begin your descent, but today we celebrate you.
All	Be with us this day.
Priestess	Lady of All, queen of summer, we welcome you in your full mother aspect as the fields begin to ripen and you awaken a spark of divine love deep in our souls.
All	Be with us this day.
Priest	Even though most of summer lies ahead, the God begins to fade as the sun starts to move away from us. Tonight we rededicate ourselves to our spiritual paths and ask for Lugh's blessings.

As the Priest speaks, the Priestess takes the basket from the altar and gives each person a marigold.

Background

Share Part I of the background information here.

Priest	This day we use marigolds to honor Lugh and ask for his blessing to further our spiritual journey.

The Priest bows before the altar and then places a flower on it, saying:

Lugh, I thank you for your many blessings and reaffirm my spiritual path.

After everyone has made their affirmation, the Priest says:

Lugh, even though you will soon fade from us, your bright spirit will remain in our hearts throughout the year. So mote it be.

All	So mote it be.

Background

Share Part II of the background information here.

The Priestess leads a free-form dancing procession that weaves around the "standing stones" in the circle. Some participants may drum and use rattles or other instruments while chanting:

We call to Lugh on Solstice Day,
Shine bright before you go away.
Sun King, Lugh, bring summer heat,
Blessed be and merry meet.

After the energy reaches a peak the Priest brings the chanting and dancing to a close, and then says:

It is time to center ourselves as we move back to the everyday world. Close your eyes; let your energy spiral down. Feel it touch the earth. Be at peace this summer day. Enjoy the warm days ahead as the Wheel of the Year turns ever onward. When you are ready, open your eyes.

Closing

Priestess   Lady of All, queen of summer, thank you, Great Mother, for the richness that unfolds around us and within us. We thank you for your presence with us this day and ask for your blessing as you depart. We bid you farewell.

All   We bid you farewell.

Priest   Sun King, lord of summer, thank you for your bright spirit. We thank you for your presence with us this day and ask for your blessing as you depart. We bid you farewell.

All   We bid you farewell.

West   Powers of water, thank you for dewy mornings and gentle rains. We thank you for your presence with us this day and ask for your blessing as you depart. We bid you farewell.

All   We bid you farewell.

South   Powers of fire, thank you for your transforming flame. We thank you for your presence with us this day and ask for your blessing as you depart. We bid you farewell.

All   We bid you farewell.

East   Powers of air, thank you for warm breezes that sweeten our summer days. We thank you for your presence with us this day and ask for your blessing as you depart. We bid you farewell.

All   We bid you farewell.

North   Powers of earth, thank you for the sensuous colors and fragrance that enrich our lives. We thank you for your presence with us this day and ask for your blessing as you depart. We bid you farewell.

All   We bid you farewell.

Priestess Take time to reflect on the season and on your spiritual journey through the summer ahead. The Wheel of the Year and of our lives continues to turn. Our circle is open; may deep peace remain with you.

All   Merry meet, merry part, and merry meet again.

Solo Ritual

Casting the Circle

As you place flowers on the ground to mark your circle (large enough to encompass your "standing stones"), say:

Spring ends and summer comes upon the land. As the days grow in warmth, I ask the Lord and Lady to awaken the sacred flame within my soul. With this fragrant circle, sacred is this space decreed.

Calling the Quarters

Go to the edge of your circle and face each direction, respectively. After speaking, light a candle on the altar. Face the altar when evoking the Goddess and God.

Speak   I look to the north and call on the powers of earth to join me in my circle. Your body sends forth the blooms of early summer with rich sensuous colors. Be with me as a bright red flower.

I look to the east and call on the powers of air to join me in my circle. Caress me with your warm breezes that sweeten my life with soft-scented flowers and plants. Be with me as the fragrant linden.

I look to the south and call on the powers of fire to join me in my circle. Your growing heat transforms the world into a lush garden. Kiss me gently with your warmth.

I look to the west and the powers of water. Your gentle rains banish thirst and wash me clean. Touch me with dew-filled mornings.

Sun King, lord of summer, I welcome you at your zenith, your last full shining. Tomorrow you begin your descent, but today I celebrate you.

Lady of All, queen of summer, I welcome you in your full mother aspect as the fields begin to ripen and you awaken a spark of divine love deep in my soul.

Stand facing your altar, and say:

This day I use marigolds to honor Lugh and ask for his blessing to further my spiritual journey.

Bow and then place a flower on the altar, saying:

Lugh, Beli Mawr, I thank you for your many blessings and reaffirm my spiritual path. Even though you will soon fade, your bright spirit will remain in my heart throughout the year. So mote it be.

Begin the taped music or do your own drumming and start a free-form dance weaving in and out among your "standing stones." Chant:

<blockquote>
I call to Lugh on Solstice Day,
Shine bright before you go away.
Sun King, Lugh, bring summer heat,
Blessed be and merry meet.
</blockquote>

Continue until you feel the energy reach a peak, and then bring the music, drumming, and chanting to a close. You may want to take time to meditate on your blessings as well as the reasons that you reaffirm your spiritual path.

Use your usual method for grounding energy or play back a recorded centering exercise.

Closing
Extinguish each altar candle before or after each devocation.

Speak   Lady of All, queen of summer, thank you, Great Mother, for the richness that unfolds around me and within me. I thank you for your presence with me this day and ask for your blessing as you depart. I bid you farewell.

Sun King, lord of summer, thank you for your bright spirit. I thank you for your presence with me this day and ask for your blessing as you depart. I bid you farewell.

Powers of water, thank you for dewy mornings and gentle rains. I thank you for your presence with me this day and ask for your blessing as you depart. I bid you farewell.

Powers of fire, thank you for your transforming flame. I thank you for your presence with me this day and ask for your blessing as you depart. I bid you farewell.

Powers of air, thank you for warm breezes that sweeten long summer days. I thank you for your presence with me this day and ask for your blessing as you depart. I bid you farewell.

Powers of earth, thank you for the sensuous colors and fragrance that enrich my life. I thank you for your presence with me this day and ask for your blessing as you depart. I bid you farewell.

And so my spiritual journey continues as the Wheel of the Year turns ever onward. As my circle is open, may deep peace remain. Blessed be.

---

1. Loreena McKennitt, *Parallel Dreams* (Quinlan Road Limited, 1994), CD.

Lughnasadh

Lughnasadh (*Lammas* in English) is the time of the first harvest, the festival of first fruits when the Sun King fades as the grain is taken from the fields. As god of the harvest and light, Lugh, king of the Tuatha de Danann, was the male counterpart to Brigid. His death, according to Edain McCoy, comes from the "belief that a god must eventually bow down to his goddess through whose benevolence he is reborn."[1]

In Scotland Lughnasadh was called *Lunasduinn*. In France the first harvest was celebrated in honor of the god Lugus. The Latin word for the town named after him was *Lugudunum* ("Lug's town"), which eventually became Lyons. Under Roman influence, the celebrations were held in honor of the emperor Augustus whose name was adapted for the month.

In August, the hot, humid weather that bathes the land in a warm haze imposes a slower pace so that plants and animals (including we humans) have time to complete the annual cycle of growth. Roses may be fading, but lavender and chamomile are in their glory. Thunderstorms bring relief from blazing temperatures and raise energy that further nourishes growing plants. Whenever possible, tap into this energy. Rituals performed during storms can be powerful experiences.

Background for This Ritual

Solo practitioners will want to read this just before starting the ritual. A place has been indicated in the group ritual where this is most appropriate for the Priestess or Priest to read to everyone:

In our modern world it is easy to forget how important a successful harvest was to our ancestors. They had cause for celebration: a good harvest meant survival in the dark, cold months ahead. A poor or bad harvest signaled the beginning of difficult times. Even though we can nip out to the supermarket whenever we need something, this is a good time to give thought to where our food originates and reverence for the cycles that produce it. Better still, tending a garden keeps us in touch with the Goddess and her bounty. Even if your garden consists only of tomatoes or herbs grown in pots on a balcony, these taste all the sweeter for having been nurtured by your own hands.

Tonight's circle is created to give thanks for what the Lord and Lady provide. The late summer harvest is a time of transformation: a time to take stock of how the year has unfolded thus far, what you have done, and what you are ready to reap. The fruits of the seeds planted in the spring—physical and spiritual—are ready to be gathered in.

Themes

- Celebrate the bounty of the earth.

- Give thanks for blessings.

- Prepare for the transition to harvesttime—both physical and spiritual.

Preparation

- Six pieces of fruit, vegetables, or a combination placed in a basket near the altar

- Chalice

- Athame

- Honey mead or other honeyed drink such as chamomile tea

- Corn bread on a plate

- Small paper cups filled with grapes, enough for each participant

FOR SOLO RITUAL
- Wand (optional)

Group Ritual

Priestess It is high summer. The days are hot and the nights sultry. The first harvest is taken in and we rejoice in the bounty that is provided.

Casting the Circle

Priestess A circle is a symbol of completeness and continuity. It is the Wheel of the Year, the cycle of life.

The Priestess takes the hand of the person to her left saying:
Hand to hand the circle is cast.

As each participant takes the hand of the person next to him or her, he or she repeats:
Hand to hand the circle is cast.

Priestess With this circle we create sacred space where the realms touch.

Calling the Quarters

Each person making an evocation, including the Priest and Priestess, takes a fruit or vegetable from the basket. Before speaking, they walk to the edge of the circle and raise the fruit/vegetable in both hands. The Priest and Priestess make their evocations standing in front of the altar. After speaking, the fruit/vegetable is placed on the altar.

North Come ye spirits of north, powers of earth, bring the beauty of ripe, golden fields. Be with us this night.

All Be with us this night.

East Come ye spirits of east, powers of air, bring the cool morning breeze. Be with us this night.

All Be with us this night.

South Come ye spirits of south, powers of fire, bring the hot, sultry summer afternoons. Be with us this night.

All Be with us this night.

West Come ye spirits of west, powers of water, bring the warm rains that nourish the fields. Be with us this night.

All	Be with us this night.
Priest	Lord Lugh, lord of the harvest, the bounty of your seed ripens in the fields and orchards. Be with us this night.
All	Be with us this night.
Priestess	Lady Gaia, mother of us all, your great swollen belly provides abundance. Nourish us, protect us. Be with us this night.
All	Be with us this night.
Priestess	We give thanks for what the Lord and Lady provide.

At the altar, the Priestess takes up the chalice and the Priest the athame. He lowers it slowly into the raised chalice to symbolize the Great Rite. In unison, they say:

> This is Lughnasadh, the time of Lugh. This is the time of the first harvest. We celebrate the bounty of Gaia and Lugh.

The Priestess fills the chalice with honey mead. The Priest takes the plate of corn bread. Beginning at the north point of the circle he places a small piece of corn bread in each participant's mouth, and the Priestess gives each a sip from the chalice. As they do so they say, respectively:

> Share the bounty of the Lord.
> Share the bounty of the Lady.

After all participants receive corn bread and mead, the Priest and Priestess minister to each other.

Background

Share the background information here.

As the Priestess speaks, the Priest gives each participant a paper cup of grapes.

Priestess	Take a look at your life. What began earlier in the year, has grown, and is ready to come fully into your life? Hold the cup of grapes between your hands. Think of what you want to reap in this time of harvest.
	When you have it firmly in your mind, eat one of the grapes, and then place one on the altar as an offering. After you have done that, move about freely with other coveners and feed grapes to each other, voicing what you wish for the other. If you know someone is having difficulty, wish that it is

resolved. Or, if you don't know someone well, you may simply wish that they be blessed with what they need.

After participants begin moving around the circle, the Priestess and Priest begin the chant:

As friends in a circle,
A gift for you,
May the Goddess grant
Your wishes true.

Participants may choose to drum and/or dance. When the energy has reached its peak, the Priest and Priestess slow the chanting and bring it to a halt.

Priestess   May our wishes and intentions be carried above and below.

All   As above, so below.

Priest   It is time to move back to our everyday world. Close your eyes and let your breath settle into a comfortable rhythm. Let go of the energy and let it spiral down. Let it bring relaxation down through your body. Let the energy flow down, down to your feet and then continue through the floor. Let your energy continue below this building. Touch your energy to Mother Earth as you come back into everyday awareness. Take a moment to reflect on what you will reap in this harvest. When you are ready, open your eyes.

Closing

Each participant faces his or her respective direction while speaking. The Priest and Priestess face the altar.

Priestess   Lady Gaia, we thank you for your blessing and presence in our circle this night. Stay if you will; go if you must. We bid thee farewell.

All   We bid thee farewell, Lady Gaia.

Priest   Lord Lugh, lord of the harvest, we thank you for your blessing and presence in our circle this night. Stay if you will; go if you must. We bid thee farewell.

All   We bid thee farewell, Lord Lugh.

West	Spirits of west, powers of water, we thank you for your blessing and presence in our circle this night. Stay if you will; go if you must. We bid thee farewell.
All	We bid thee farewell, spirits of west.
South	Spirits of south, powers of fire, we thank you for your blessing and presence in our circle this night. Stay if you will; go if you must. We bid thee farewell.
All	We bid thee farewell, spirits of south.
East	Spirits of east, powers of air, we thank you for your blessing and presence in our circle this night. Stay if you will; go if you must. We bid thee farewell.
All	We bid thee farewell, spirits of east.
North	Spirits of north, powers of earth, we thank you for your blessing and presence in our circle this night. Stay if you will; go if you must. We bid thee farewell.
All	We bid thee farewell, spirits of north.

Everyone joins hands around the circle.

Priestess	As all good things must sometimes end, Go forth with the love the Goddess sends. For if your heart is always true, This circle will come back to you.
All	Merry meet, merry part, and merry meet again. Blessed be.

Solo Ritual

Casting the Circle

With your athame or wand, walk the perimeter of your circle.

Speak	A circle is a symbol of completeness and continuity. It is the Wheel of the Year, the cycle of life. Now is high summer. The days are hot and the nights

are sultry. The first harvest is taken in and I rejoice in the bounty that is provided.

When you arrive back where you started, say:

With this circle sacred space has been created where the realms touch.

Calling the Quarters

Take a fruit or vegetable from the basket. Before speaking, walk to the edge of the circle and raise it in both hands. For the Lord and Lady, make evocations standing in front of the altar. After speaking, place the fruit/vegetable on the altar.

Speak   Come ye spirits of north, powers of earth, bring the beauty of ripe, golden fields. Be with me this night.

Come ye spirits of east, powers of air, bring the cool morning breeze. Be with me this night.

Come ye spirits of south, powers of fire, bring the hot, sultry summer afternoons. Be with me this night.

Come ye spirits of west, powers of water, bring the warm rains that nourish the fields. Be with me this night.

Lord Lugh, lord of the harvest, the bounty of your seed ripens in the fields and orchards. Be with me this night.

Lady Gaia, mother of all, your great swollen belly provides abundance. Nourish me, protect me. Be with me this night.

At the altar, take up the chalice and the athame. Slowly lower the athame into the raised chalice to symbolize the Great Rite, saying:

This is Lughnasadh, the time of Lugh. This is the time of the first harvest. I celebrate the bounty of Gaia and Lugh.

Fill the chalice with honey mead. Before taking a bite of corn bread and a sip of mead say, respectively:

I share the bounty of the Lord.

I share the bounty of the Lady.

Think of what began earlier in the year, has grown, and is ready to come to fruition in your life. Take the cup of grapes and hold it between your hands. Think of what you want to reap in this time of harvest. When you have it firmly in your mind, eat one of the grapes, and then place one on the altar as an offering. After you have done that, you may want to move about your circle and voice what you wish for others. If you know someone is having difficulty, wish that it is resolved. You may also want to send loving energy to the earth and out into the world.

To add energy to your wishes, drum, dance, and chant:

> With my circle I send a gift to you,
> May the Goddess grant your wishes true.

When the energy has reached its peak, slow your chanting, bring it to a halt, and then say:
> May my wishes and intentions be carried above and below.

Use your usual method for grounding and centering or play back a tape of the one in the group ritual.

Closing

Face each direction respectively from that point in your circle. Stand in front of the altar for the Lord and Lady.

Speak   Lady Gaia, thank you for your blessing and presence in my circle this night. Stay if you will; go if you must. I bid thee farewell.

Lord Lugh, lord of the harvest, thank you for your blessing and presence in my circle this night. Stay if you will; go if you must. I bid thee farewell.

Spirits of west, powers of water, thank you for your blessing and presence in my circle this night. Stay if you will; go if you must. I bid thee farewell.

Spirits of south, powers of fire, thank you for your blessing and presence in my circle this night. Stay if you will; go if you must. I bid thee farewell.

Spirits of east, powers of air, thank you for your blessing and presence in my circle this night. Stay if you will; go if you must. I bid thee farewell.

Spirits of north, powers of earth, thank you for your blessing and presence in my circle this night. Stay if you will; go if you must. I bid thee farewell.

As all good things must sometimes end,
Go forth with the love the Goddess sends.
For if your heart is always true,
This circle will come back to you.

---

1. Edain McCoy, *Witta: An Irish Pagan Tradition* (St. Paul, MN: Llewellyn Publications, 1993), 194–95.

Mabon

M abon, the second of the three major harvests, is also the autumn equinox. Like its spring counterpart, this is a day of balance between light and dark, but the bright summer sun will soon be overtaken by darkness as the days grow short. This marks the Sun King's/Corn King's descent to the underworld, his return to the Goddess's womb from which he will be reborn at Yule.

This time of year brings a harvest of carrots, parsnips, and beets. Fruits and vegetables that grow on vines are ripening and ready to harvest. It is also time to harvest blackberries (a fruit sacred to Brigid), which are used to make wine in the British Isles where grapes do not always fare well.

If you have a garden (large plot or containers on a small porch), give thought to its wonders. Spend time with your garden. Enjoy the plants that provide food and flavorings, or sweeten the air. Your energy nourishes them. Sing or chant as you tend and harvest, and you will be rewarded.

Background for This Ritual

Solo practitioners will want to read this just before beginning the ritual. A place has been indicated in the group ritual where this is most appropriate for the Priestess or Priest to read to everyone, or it can be read before beginning:

> This is Mabon, the time of the second harvest. We enjoy a wealth of good
> food and weather that is neither too hot nor too cold. Beauty surrounds us

as autumn colors begin to blaze. We reap the beauty and bounty of this earth. We also reap the fruit of the seeds we have symbolically sown in our lives this year. Tonight we take time to count our blessings and give thanks to the Lord and Lady.

Themes

- Give thanks for abundance and blessings.

- Celebrate the beauty of autumn.

- Bid farewell to the God.

Dance

The vine dance can be done in both group and solo rituals because it is the dance step that creates the "vine."

To move deosil, your left leg will advance your step. Your right leg will move first, behind then in front of the left to simulate the winding growth of a vine. Place your right foot behind the left, then step sideways with your left foot. Cross your right foot in front of the left, and then take another step with your left foot. Keep alternating the movement of your right foot behind, then in front of your left.

For the group ritual, everyone joins hands either downward forming a V or up (bending at the elbows) forming a W.

Preparation

Items for this ritual include the following:

- Two brown or yellow candles for the altar

- Chalice and small paper cups for people who prefer not to drink from the chalice

- A basket of apples with one apple for each participant in group ritual, or enough apples for the circle boundary in solo ritual

- Three additional apples

- A sharp knife to cut the apples

- A basket of gourds with one gourd for each participant

- Blackberry wine or juice

- A small bowl of hazelnuts

- Vines (real or from a craft store) to decorate your altar (optional)

- Drum (optional)

Group Ritual

Priestess   The days are still warm with the remnants of summer, but at night there's a chill in the air. This is Mabon, a time to give thanks to the Goddess for her bounty and blessings. This is a time to pause and enjoy the magic and beauty of the earth. Tonight is peaceful, but change is in the wind.

Casting the Circle

The Priest takes up the basket of apples from the altar and walks deosil around the circle handing one to each participant.

Priestess   Tonight we cast our circle with the apple, an ancient symbol of the Goddess with her great knowledge and power of healing. The apple tree itself is known as the custodian of her wisdom. And it is the apple tree that provides a gateway into other realms.

Hold your apple in both hands. Feel the wisdom and love of the Goddess. Now, raise your arms and lift this nurturing fruit in honor of the Great Mother.

As above, so below. We form our circle with her bounty.

Participants place the apples on the ground behind them.

We have created sacred space with the riches of the Great Mother's body.

Calling the Quarters

The Priestess cuts two apples in half across their middles, and says:

This sacred fruit contains the five-pointed star, the symbol of our ancient faith and connectedness to all life.

She hands half an apple to each participant prior to their calling a direction. In turn, they place the half apple at the edge of the circle in the respective directions.

North   Spirits of north, element earth, your golden fields provide the promise of a comfortable winter. Let us celebrate in the abundance of your blessings. Join us in our circle this night.

All   Join us this night.

East   Spirits of east, element air, your warm summer breezes yield to the autumn chill that gives birth to a blaze of bright color. Let us appreciate the blessings of the beauty you bestow on this world. Join us in our circle this night.

All   Join us this night.

South   Spirits of south, element fire, your brilliant August sun is becoming a memory that will dance through our hearts in the dark months to come. May we find your spark to illuminate our path ahead. Join us in our circle this night.

All   Join us this night.

West   Spirits of west, element water, your cool autumn rains wash the emptying fields to make way for a winter's rest. May we receive the blessing of your cleansing showers. Join us in our circle this night.

All   Join us this night.

The Priestess cuts another apple in half. She keeps one half and hands the other to the Priest. He holds it above the altar.

Priest   Sun King, Corn King, god of the harvest, your seed has provided a bounty that has greened the meadows and filled the fields. As the burning embers of summer are overtaken by darkness and you begin your descent to the underworld, bestow your blessings on this circle.

All   Join us this night.

He places the half apple on the altar and lights one of the two candles.

The Priestess holds the other half apple above the altar, and says:

> Great Mother Goddess, Brigid, Demeter, queen of the harvest, your body has provided abundance and beauty. As you begin your metamorphosis into crone, bless us with your wisdom.

All   Join us this night.

She places the half apple on the altar and lights the other candle. The Priest and Priestess join hands and in unison say:

> Lord and Lady of the Harvest, as this year wanes into darkness, come to us one last time as Queen and Consort. Join us in our circle this night.

All   Join us this night.

Background

Share the background information here if it was not read before starting the ritual.

Priestess   Take a moment or two and give thought to what you have been blessed with this year. When you are ready, go to the altar and take a gourd from the basket. With both hands raise the gourd above the altar, and say, "Lord and Lady, I thank you for," then state the blessing that you have received. You may also choose to hold your blessing in the privacy of your heart and simply say, "Lord and Lady, I thank you for this blessing."

During this time the Priest, Priestess, or a helper may drum softly. After all participants have given thanks, the Priestess and Priest take their turns.

Priestess   To give power to our thanks as we release them to the world, we raise energy with the vine dance.

Provide explanation of dance steps. Some participants may choose to drum instead of dance. The following chant is used while dancing:

> Harvest dance, go round and round,
> With blessings for all to be found.

The Priestess brings the dancing and chanting to an end after it has reached its peak and the energy released.

Priestess   You may want to sit on the floor, or put your hands on the floor. Take time to let your energy flow down through your body, down through you and into the earth. Touch your energy to Mother Earth. Feel her balance bring you to center.

We now pass from summer into the dark of the year. On this day of the equinox, this day of balance, we pause on the threshold where light begins to fade. As the nights grow longer we take time to reflect on our lives and cultivate inner wisdom.

The Priest raises the bowl of hazelnuts, saying:

Hazel is a symbol of wisdom. We call on the wise ones to guide us through the dark that lies ahead. Teach us to hear the inner voice that whispers of ancient ways.

The Priestess raises the wine, saying:

Blackberries, fruit sacred to Brigid, sweeten our lips and warm our hearts with memories of this summer past.

The Priest and Priestess perform the Great Rite, lowering the athame into the chalice. In unison they say:

The Horned One returns to the belly of the mother.
The Great Goddess transforms into the powerful crone.
We follow them into darkness, as two become one.
The seasons change, the Wheel of the Year turns.

The Priestess pours the wine into the chalice and says:

Mother, bless this wine and food.

The Priest takes the bowl of hazelnuts. Beginning in the north sector of the circle, the Priest places a hazelnut in each participant's mouth, saying:

May you never hunger.

The Priestess gives each participant a sip of wine, saying:

May you never thirst.

When they have gone around the circle, they share hazelnuts and wine.

Priestess   We look ahead to the darkness for rest and renewal.

Closing

Priestess   Great Mother, as you enter your most powerful aspect of crone, we ask that you favor us with your wisdom. Guide us through the coming dark. We bid you farewell.

All   We bid you farewell. Blessed be.

The Priestess extinguishes a candle.

Priest   Horned One, warrior of light, go to your rest and dream of rebirth. Endings are beginnings. We shall await your return. We bid you farewell.

All   We bid you farewell. Blessed be.

The Priest extinguishes a candle.

Each person in turn picks up the half apple he or she placed at the edge of the circle, and then places it on the altar after speaking.

West   Spirits of west, element water, thank you for your presence this night. Stay if you will; go if you must. We bid you farewell.

All   We bid you farewell. Blessed be.

South   Spirits of south, element fire, thank you for your presence this night. Stay if you will; go if you must. We bid you farewell.

All   We bid you farewell. Blessed be.

East   Spirits of east, element air, thank you for your presence this night. Stay if you will; go if you must. We bid you farewell.

All   We bid you farewell. Blessed be.

North   Spirits of north, element earth, thank you for your presence this night. Stay if you will; go if you must. We bid you farewell.

All   We bid you farewell. Blessed be.

Each participant picks up the apple he or she placed on the floor and holds it in front of him- or herself.

Priestess	The Lord has gone to his rest, and the Lady gathers strength. We witness their parting as the Wheel of the Year continues to turn.
All	Merry meet, merry part, and merry meet again. Blessed be.

Solo Ritual

Casting the Circle

Take an apple from the basket and hold it in both hands. Feel the wisdom and love of the Goddess; feel her generosity. Walking deosil, place apples on the floor to mark your circle as you say:

This is an ancient symbol of the Goddess with her great knowledge and power of healing. It holds her wisdom and provides a gateway into other realms. As above, so below. Sacred is this space decreed with the riches of the Great Mother's body.

Calling the Quarters

Cut two apples in half across their middles.

Speak	This sacred fruit contains the five-pointed star, the symbol of my ancient faith and connectedness to all life.

Place half an apple at the edge of the circle in the respective directions after speaking.

Speak	Spirits of north, element earth, your golden fields provide the promise of a comfortable winter. I celebrate in the abundance of your blessings. Join me in my circle this night.
	Spirits of east, element air, your warm summer breezes yield to the autumn chill that gives birth to a blaze of bright color. I appreciate the blessings of the beauty you bestow on this world. Join me in my circle this night.
	Spirits of south, element fire, your brilliant August sun is becoming a memory that will dance through my heart in the dark months to come. May I find your spark to illuminate my path ahead. Join me in my circle this night.
	Spirits of west, element water, your cool autumn rains wash the emptying fields to make way for a winter's rest. May I receive the blessing of your cleansing showers. Join me in my circle this night.

Cut another apple in half. Hold one half at a time as you call the Goddess and God. After speaking, place it on the altar and light a candle.

Speak   Sun King, Corn King, god of the harvest, your seed has provided a bounty that has greened the meadows and filled the fields. As the burning embers of summer are overtaken by darkness and you begin your descent to the underworld, bestow your blessings on my circle.

Great Mother Goddess, Brigid, Demeter, queen of the harvest, your body has provided abundance and beauty. As you begin your metamorphosis into crone, bless me with your wisdom.

Lord and Lady of the Harvest, as this year wanes into darkness, come to me one last time as Queen and Consort. Join me in my circle this night.

Take a moment or two and give thought to what you have been blessed with this year. When you are ready, go to the altar and take a gourd from the basket. With both hands raise the gourd above the altar, and say:

Lord and Lady, I thank you for _____ [*state the blessings you have received*].

To give power to your thanks as you release it to the world, raise energy with the vine dance. As you move around the circle, chant:

Harvest dance, go round and round,
With blessings for all to be found.

After the energy has reached its peak and has been released, bring your dancing and chanting to an end. Take a few moments to ground your energy.

Speak   My world passes from summer into the dark of the year. On this day of the equinox, this day of balance, I pause on the threshold where light begins to fade. As the nights grow longer it is time to reflect on my life and cultivate inner wisdom.

Raise the bowl of hazelnuts, saying:

Hazel is a symbol of wisdom. I call on the wise ones to guide me through the dark that lies ahead. Teach me to hear the inner voice that whispers of ancient ways.

Raise the wine, saying:

> Blackberries, fruit sacred to Brigid, sweeten my lips and warm my heart with memories of this summer past.

Perform the Great Rite, lowering the athame into the chalice, saying:

> The Horned One returns to the belly of the mother.
> The Great Goddess transforms into the powerful crone.
> I follow them into darkness, as two become one.
> The seasons change, the Wheel of the Year turns.

Pour the wine into the chalice, saying:

> Mother, bless this wine and food.

Before taking a bite of the hazelnuts and a sip of wine say, respectively:

> May I never hunger.
> May I never thirst.

Speak   I look ahead to the darkness for rest and renewal.

Closing

Speak   Great Mother, as you enter your most powerful aspect of crone, I ask that you favor me with your wisdom. Guide me through the coming dark. I bid you farewell.

Extinguish one of the candles.

Speak   Horned One, warrior of light, go to your rest and dream of rebirth. Endings are beginnings. I shall await your return. I bid you farewell.

Extinguish the other candle. Pick up the half apple placed at the edge of the circle for each direction, and then place it on the altar after speaking.

Speak   Spirits of west, element water, thank you for your presence this night. Stay if you will; go if you must. I bid you farewell.

Spirits of south, element fire, thank you for your presence this night. Stay if you will; go if you must. I bid you farewell.

Spirits of east, element air, thank you for your presence this night. Stay if you will; go if you must. I bid you farewell.

Spirits of north, element earth, thank you for your presence this night. Stay if you will; go if you must. I bid you farewell.

The Lord has gone to his rest, and the Lady gathers strength. I witness their parting as the Wheel of the Year continues to turn. In faith and unity, blessed be.

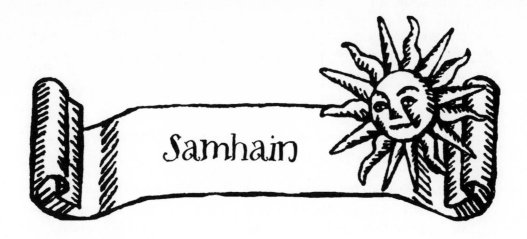

Samhain

amhain is a time to remember ancestors and invite their spirits to come close. Legends of evil spirits on the prowl this night is a misrepresentation of the belief that the barrier between the worlds of the seen and unseen is thin. It was the custom in Europe to place candles in the windows to help ancestors find their way. This developed into the jack-o'-lantern, which was intended to welcome and guide as well as warn any unwanted spirits to stay away.

In many parts of the British Isles, Samhain marked the beginning of the winter half of the year. Before the dark of the year began, it was important to have the final harvest gathered in. Anything not harvested by October 30 remained in the fields.

It was also customary to celebrate and hold a feast for the dead. (The Christian church later fashioned it into the Feast of All Saints.) The feast could be a complete meal with an extra place set for the dead, or it could be as simple as leaving cakes and wine by the fireside.

The hazelnut is associated with Samhain because it is one of the last things to be harvested. The hazel tree itself was revered by the Celtic peoples as a symbol of wisdom and divination. It is customary to string nine hazelnuts together (hazel is the ninth month in the Celtic tree calendar), tie the ends together, and consecrate it in the smoke of the Samhain fire. The hazelnut ring is then hung in the house as a protective amulet for the coming year.

This is the time when the Goddess is in her full crone aspect. She represents winter and death, which is necessary for future renewal. The death/regeneration aspect of this time of year is signified by animals going into hibernation. For humans, it's a time for personal study and introspection in preparation for the new cycle that begins at Yule. It is our own symbolic death before renewal.

Background for This Ritual

Solo practitioners will want to read this just before beginning the ritual. A place has been indicated in the group ritual where this is most appropriate for the Priestess or Priest to read to everyone:

> **Part I:** Samhain is a time of transition as the earth prepares for winter's rest and we prepare for our journey through the dark of the year. Samhain is a time to reflect and remember ancestors, loved ones, including pets, who no longer walk this earth. It is important to remember them and speak their names.

> **Part II:** Samhain is a time of transition when we begin our journey through the dark of the year. Just as Persephone descended to the underworld to guide the spirits of the departed, so we descend into ourselves to find the path our spirits need to follow.
>
> This year has waxed with the fullness of life and now wanes into shadow. Our souls take rest in the dark as the wheel of the seasons makes its final turn.

Cord Magic

Solo practitioners will want to read this before beginning the ritual. A place has been indicated in the group ritual where this is most appropriate for the Priestess or Priest to explain this to everyone:

> Take three strands of yarn, one of each color (see the "Preparation" section). Very slowly, twine them together. You can braid them or simply knot them together. Tie at least three knots. If you want to use more knots, do so in multiples of three. Work your love into the yarn. When you have finished, hold the yarn between your palms and send your energy to your loved ones. They will feel your warmth.

Themes

- Remember those who have passed beyond the veil.
- Prepare for your inward journey through winter.

Preparation

Items for this ritual include the following:

- Two white candles and four black candles

- Four small sprigs of bittersweet

- One branch of bittersweet

- Strands of black, white, and red yarn cut to twelve-inch lengths placed in a basket on the altar

- Pomegranate seeds in a bowl

FOR SOLO RITUAL
- One piece of candy

Group Ritual

Priestess   At night there's a chill in the air. The leaves of trees have blazed to their full autumn splendor and are drifting away on the wind. This is the time of Hecate, Cerridwen, the Dark Mother who stands alone. This is the time to contemplate the cycle of life, death, and rebirth for tonight the veil between the worlds is thin.

Casting the Circle

Priestess   We cast our circle by passing a branch of bittersweet, for tonight is bittersweet with thoughts of those we love who have passed to Tir-na-nog.

The Priestess passes the branch to her right. Each participant slowly passes it on. When it has gone around the circle, the Priestess continues:

The circle is cast. This is hallowed ground, and we are between the worlds of the seen and unseen.

Calling the Quarters

Each person who is evoking a direction will have a small sprig of bittersweet before the ritual begins. After speaking, the participant places the sprig on the altar beside the black candle he or she will light.

North	We look to the north, place of silent caverns. Spirits of earth, you nourish us in life and wrap your welcoming body around us in death. Gather here in the name of Inanna, in the name of Tammuz. Be with us this night.
All	Be with us this night.
East	We set our gaze to the east, source of breath. Spirits of air, you are with us at the beginning and depart with us when we leave this realm. Be with us in the name of Astarte, in the name of Dumuzi. Be with us this night.
All	Be with us this night.
South	We call to the south, source of transforming flame. Spirits of fire, your brilliant spark guides us through the cycles of life. Come in the name of Hestia, in the name of Horus. Be with us this night.
All	Be with us this night.
West	We turn to the west, place of deep wells and underground springs. Spirits of water, you carry us through the ebbs and flows of life on your never-ending tides. Join us in the name of Isis, in the name of Osiris. Be with us this night.
All	Be with us this night.

The Priestess places the branch of bittersweet that was used to cast the circle on the altar after lighting one of the white candles.

Priestess	Dark Mother, you come to us alone this night in mourning for your son, in mourning for your consort. The God has departed to the underworld and the Wheel of the Year follows him into darkness. Crone of the ages, we call on you, be with us this night.
All	Be with us this night.

Background

Share Part I of the background information here.

The Priestess lights the other white candle, and says:

We take time to honor those we love, those who have gone before. In remembrance we speak their names.

After naming those she wants to remember, the Priestess passes the candle to the person on her left. Each participant speaks the name(s) of the person(s) he or she wishes to honor. When the candle returns to the Priestess she raises it above the altar, saying:

Hecate, Cerridwen, guide the spirits of those named here this night.

The Priest or a helper takes the basket of yarn from the altar and gives three strands to each participant.

Priestess   We take time to honor those we have named and to celebrate their lives. Hold in your mind the memories of those whose names you have spoken. Think of how they have touched your life. Feel their presence with you in this hallowed circle.

Cord Magic

Share the cord magic information here.

Priestess   As you work with the yarn/cord, join me in chanting:

Mother of Darkness, these names we share;
Of those we love now in your care.
Guide them gently with love so sweet;
Blessed be until we meet.

When all participants have had time to finish braiding the yarn and hold it while singing, the Priestess slowly brings the chant to a halt.

Priestess   When you go home tonight, place the yarn on your altar or some special place. Set a piece of candy with it. This will carry the intention to sweeten your loved one's journey into their next life.

Background

Share Part II of the background information here.

The Priestess takes the bowl of pomegranate seeds from the altar. Going to each participant, she squeezes the pomegranate seeds, and with a finger places a drop of the juice on his or her lips, saying:

May your spirit find its path.

When she has completed the circuit, the Priest or a helper places a drop of juice on the Priestess's lips and repeats the phrase.

Priestess   It is time to bid farewell to the spirits of our loved ones as we begin to move back to our everyday world. Close your eyes and take time to let your energy flow down through your body. Down through you and into the earth. Touch your energy to Mother Earth. Feel her balance bring you to center.

Closing

Priestess   Dark Mother, ancient and enduring one, guide us, watch over us and our loved ones both here and departed. We stand at this gateway with you and thank you for your gifts of restoration and renewal. Blessed be.

All   Blessed be, Dark Mother.

The Priestess extinguishes both white candles. Each person, in turn, extinguishes the black candle he or she lit after dismissing his or her direction.

West   Water of Life, you sustain us before birth and nourish us as we grow. Spirits of water, we thank you for your presence this night. Stay if you will; go if you must. Blessed be.

All   Blessed be, Water of Life.

South   Fire of Renewal, like a brilliant sun you warm us and remain forever a guiding light. Spirits of fire, we thank you for your presence this night. Stay if you will; go if you must. Blessed be.

All   Blessed be, Fire of Renewal.

East   Breath of Life, you carry us through our lives as a constant companion to the rhythm of our hearts. Spirits of air, we thank you for your presence this night. Stay if you will; go if you must. Blessed be.

All	Blessed be, Breath of Life.
North	Mother Earth, at our journey's end may we return to rest in your loving cradle. Spirits of earth, we thank you for your presence this night. Stay if you will; go if you must. Blessed be.
All	Blessed be, Mother Earth.

Everyone joins hands around the circle.

Priestess	If we fear death we cannot fully live, and if we fear life we will not find solace in death. Every beginning has an ending and every ending has a beginning. The Wheel of the Year turns as do the cycles of our lives. Blessed be.
All	Blessed be.

Solo Ritual

Casting the Circle

Holding the branch of bittersweet, walk widdershins (counterclockwise) around your circle, saying:

> Tonight I cast my circle with bittersweet for tonight is bittersweet with thoughts of those I love who have passed to Tir-na-nog.
>
> This is the time of Hecate, Cerridwen, the Dark Mother who stands alone. This is the time to contemplate the cycle of life, death, and rebirth for tonight the veil between the worlds is thin. The circle is cast. Hallowed is this space decreed.

Place the branch of bittersweet on the altar.

Calling the Quarters

Place a sprig of bittersweet at the edge of your circle before calling each direction. Light a black candle after speaking.

Speak	I look to the north, place of silent caverns. Spirits of earth, you nourish me in life and wrap your welcoming body around me in death. Gather here in the name of Inanna, in the name of Tammuz. Be with me this night.

I set my gaze to the east, source of breath. Spirits of air, you are with me at the beginning and depart with me when I leave this realm. Be with me in the name of Astarte, in the name of Dumuzi. Be with me this night.

I call to the south, source of transforming flame. Spirits of fire, your brilliant spark guides me through the cycles of life. Come in the name of Hestia, in the name of Horus. Be with me this night.

I turn to the west, place of deep wells and underground springs. Spirits of water, you carry me through the ebbs and flows of life on your never-ending tides. Join me in the name of Isis, in the name of Osiris. Be with me this night.

Light one of the white candles after saying:

Dark Mother, you come to me alone this night in mourning for your son, in mourning for your consort. The God has departed to the underworld and the Wheel of the Year follows him into darkness. Crone of the ages, I call on you, be with me this night.

Light the other white candle, and say:

I take time to honor those I love, those who have gone before. In remembrance I speak their names.

Say the names of those you want to remember, then continue:

Hecate, Cerridwen, guide the spirits of those named here this night.

Take time to honor those you have named and to celebrate their lives. Hold in your mind the memories of those whose names you spoke. Think of how they have touched your life. Feel their presence with you in this hallowed circle.

Cord Magic

As you work with the cord/yarn, chant:

> Mother of Darkness, these names I share;
> Of those I love now in your care.
> Guide them gently with love so sweet;
> Blessed be until we meet.

When you finish chanting, place the yarn on your altar. Set the piece of candy with it. This will carry the intention to sweeten your loved ones' journey into their next life.

Take the bowl of pomegranate seeds from the altar. Lift it and say:

> This year has waxed with the fullness of life and now wanes into shadow. My soul will take rest in the dark as the wheel of the seasons makes its final turn.

Squeeze the pomegranate seeds, and with a finger place a drop of the juice on your lips, then say:

> May my spirit find its path.

Take time to contemplate the dark months ahead and how it can be a time of renewal for you. Use your usual method of grounding.

Closing

Speak   Dark Mother, ancient and enduring one, guide me, watch over me and my loved ones both here and departed. I stand at this gateway with you and thank you for your gifts of restoration and renewal. Blessed be.

Extinguish both white candles. In turn, extinguish the black candles.

Speak   Water of Life, you sustain me before birth and nourish me as I grow. Spirits of water, thank you for your presence this night. Stay if you will; go if you must. Blessed be.

Fire of Renewal, like a brilliant sun you warm me and remain forever a guiding light. Spirits of fire, thank you for your presence this night. Stay if you will; go if you must. Blessed be.

Breath of Life, you carry me through my life as a constant companion to the rhythm of my heart. Spirits of air, thank you for your presence this night. Stay if you will; go if you must. Blessed be.

Mother Earth, at my journey's end may I return to rest in your loving cradle. Spirits of earth, thank you for your presence this night. Stay if you will; go if you must. Blessed be.

If I fear death I cannot fully live, and if I fear life I will not find solace in death. Every beginning has an ending and every ending has a beginning. The cycles of my life continue in faith and unity with the love of the Goddess. Blessed be.

Part II

The Esbats

People began tracking time approximately 27,000 years ago by marking the thirteen annual lunations of the moon. Around 6,000 years ago, people erected great stone monuments such as Stonehenge and massive alignments of standing stones that did more than trace a year's passing. They actually tracked the 18.61 years of the lunar cycle as well as its complete triple period of 55.83 years.

Moonlight has held people in a certain enchantment, about which poets have expounded for centuries. Even to walk in the moonlight is to feel a touch of magic—one cannot help but sense the energy. Luna does not give us a harsh bright light as does the sun. She provides just enough to part the darkness of night and invite us into other realms.

The moon has two primary phases: waxing (dark or new moon to full) and waning (full to dark). (See Figure 3 for the eight named phases.) Some people celebrate only the full moons and others celebrate both dark and full.

The waning phase is a time for turning inward and reflecting. It is a time for reaping what was put forth in the waxing phase of the moon. The waning phase is often used for banishing rituals. The dark moon is a quiet time, a time for divination and personal workings. The dark moon is a time for holding power.

The waxing phase is a time for growth. It is a time to plant—literally and symbolically. Magic done during this time culminates on the full moon. This phase is conducive for creativity because of the high energy and clarity of vision it brings. It is also conducive for teaching. The energy of the full moon is intense. It is a time for sending forth intentions because of the high-powered energy that can propel them to manifest.

The esbats relate the advancing seasons with the magic of moonsheen. Even though the full moon rises at sunset on the opposite horizon from the sun, her mood reflects the seasons without being completely tethered to them. The sabbats have their traditional purposes but the esbats can run free. The energy is vibrant. Esbats are a time to laugh from the belly and dance like there is no tomorrow.

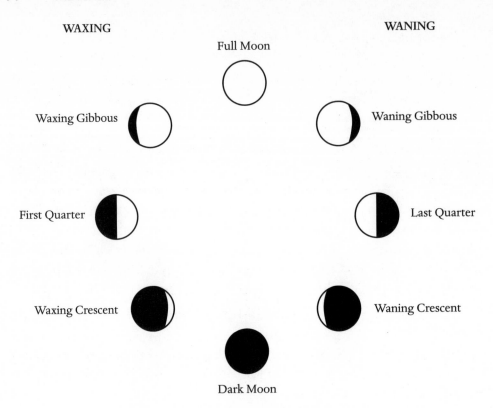

WAXING   **WANING**

Full Moon

Waxing Gibbous   Waning Gibbous

First Quarter   Last Quarter

Waxing Crescent   Waning Crescent

Dark Moon

Figure 3—The eight named phases of the moon

January

In the night of the year we are compelled to find the inner strength that will hold us and carry us to spring. It is a time for working with our inner power to develop a sense of who we are as well as to find our place in the web of existence. Winter storms may howl, but appreciating the beauty of this fierce side of nature means that we can flow with and enjoy the spiral of life energy rather than struggle against it.

Other Names for This Moon

- Wolf Moon

- Chaste Moon

- Ice Moon

In the Celtic Tree Calendar

January 1–20: Birch—associated with new beginnings, the birth/rebirth of the sun, protection, and purification.

January 21–31: Rowan—associated with the coming of new life born from the dark of winter, protection, and strength.

Background for This Ritual

This ritual is a guided meditation that includes time for journeying on your own. Solo practitioners will want to record this and insert music or leave a silent gap for the journeying segment. In a group, the Priest or Priestess may want to drum or hum softly during this time.

Summer is a fond memory and autumn's splendor has turned dull brown and gray. The hardest part of winter lies ahead even though the days are lengthening with the promise of spring and renewal.

But now it is winter. This is the time of year when many animals hibernate. For us, winter is the time for turning inward to take stock of our spiritual journey during the previous twelve months and to prepare for the year ahead so that we will emerge with spring's lifeforce knowing where we have been and where we intend to travel.

Now is the time to deepen your winter journey, your self-work. This night is the time to seek the place within you that is pure being, where you are both student and teacher. Learn to listen to your inner voice however it may reveal itself to you. It becomes easier to hear that voice as snow covers the ground and our world becomes a little quieter. Winter brings the power of silence. The light in our homes becomes a little softer as we may favor candles over electric bulbs on some evenings.

The fields are empty and the earth seems dead, but the magic of this season can be seen in the evergreens. These magnificent trees are vital and strong while everything around them seems to fade. The dark needles of the yew symbolize the death of the year that has just ended and of the things in ourselves that it is time to leave behind. The bright green needles of the fir tree represent the birth of this New Year and the parts of ourselves that we want to bring out or renew. The sacred holly with glorious shiny leaves that protect clusters of red berries is fashioned into wreaths—a circle—the Wheel of the Year. We each live this wheel in our own way and in our own journey.

During winter, this time of darkness, the days are still short and the nights long. Moonlight glitters on the frosty ground, but the air tingles with energy. The brisk air catches your breath. Think of the crystalline night sky. It may be filled with rushing snow or a few drifting flakes, or it may be sharp and clear with pinpoints of starlight. The bracing air tingles. It moves and stirs something within you.

You can feel this sky energy above your head. Reach out with your own energy, out to the beautiful night sky above. Feel its energy vibrating against your scalp. As you reach out to it, you can feel your own energy vibrate with the rhythm of the universe.

Let this energy come inside you. Let it enter your head and move down your neck to your shoulders. Feel your skin and muscles come alive. The clear, crisp winter sky is part of you. Let it move down through your chest and arms, through your stomach and abdomen. As it continues to move through your hips, legs, and feet, you can feel the lightness of the energy as it now moves with your own flow of energy. There is a continuous wave of movement from the sky. Feel it circulate through you in an endless stream.

Your entire body may feel light and free as though it could float like a snowflake. Sky energy is buoyant and can help you remain above the potential trials and tribulations of the winter months. Let it help you prepare your winter's journey. With it you will know that you can travel on whatever path you see for yourself.

As you take this time to seek the way ahead, you may encounter guides who will assist you. They may speak to you or they may take you places and show you things. They will help you learn about yourself, and perhaps tell you what you need to do in the forthcoming year or what you need to do to solve a problem.

Alternatively, you may feel yourself in a familiar place without any guides. What you see or do there will also teach or show you something that may help you in your winter's self-work. Or you may simply experience a feeling or have an image enter your mind that will aid you in self-discovery. These are only some of the ways that your own true spirit may reach out to your conscious mind. Now, follow the flow of the energy. Let it show you the way.

If you are using music or a drumming tape/CD, begin it now. Allow at least fifteen or twenty minutes before saying:

Slowly bring your awareness back to this room, back to the everyday world. Thank any guides for their help in assisting you, and bid them farewell. As the energy winds down, you may still feel light and buoyant. Become aware of your feet on the floor. Send energy through the floor into the ground. Connect with Mother Earth by giving her your sky energy. When you feel comfortable and grounded, stop sending energy. Breathe consciously as you move back to this realm. When you are ready, open your eyes.

What you may have learned or encountered may not be clear to you immediately, and it may take a day or two or maybe longer to understand. Be patient, this is part of your journey.

Themes

- Accept the fierce side of winter and connect with sky energy.

- Take time to assess your path with an inward journey.

Preparation

Items needed for this ritual include the following:

- Six candles for the altar

- White altar cloth

- Stars: Christmas ornaments in the shape of stars, star-shaped glitter, etc.

- Other symbols of winter that hold meaning for you

- Mats, pillows, or blankets for participants who may want to lie or sit on the floor during the meditation

- Meditative music or drumming tape/CD (optional)

FOR SOLO RITUAL

- Tape recorder/player

- Athame or wand

Group Ritual

Priestess   This is the Moon of the First Circle. The world seems still and silent, but under the snow-covered fields seeds rest in darkness and wait for the coming of spring. We meet in the deep night of the year to further our inward journey.

Casting the Circle

The Priestess takes the hand of the person to her left, saying:
Hand to hand the circle is cast.

As each participant takes the hand of the person next to him or her, he or she repeats:
Hand to hand the circle is cast.

Priestess   With this first circle of the year we create sacred space where the realms touch.

Calling the Quarters

Each participant walks to the edge of the circle in his or her respective direction. After speaking, he or she lights a candle on the altar. The Priest and Priestess stand in front of the altar to evoke the Goddess and God.

North   Hail, spirits of north, of earth wrapped in slumber. Below the snow and ice you rest and wait for the time of awakening. Be with us this night.

All   Be with us this night.

East   Hail, spirits of east, of air shrouded with winter fog. Your blanket of white brings a quiet stillness to the world. Be with us this night.

All   Be with us this night.

South   Hail, spirits of south, of fire warm and inviting. Keep alive the spark of life that sleeps within Mother Gaia. Be with us this night.

All   Be with us this night.

West   Hail, spirits of west, of water suspended like diamonds in winter's icy hand. Hold your secrets until you flow again. Be with us this night.

All   Be with us this night.

Priest   Hail, Lord of Winter, harsh and challenging. Your driving storms bring both beauty and danger. Your lessons we must learn. Be with us this night.

All   Be with us this night.

Priestess	Hail, Lady of Darkness, of star-studded heavens. Your crisp cold nights vibrate with the silvery gift of Luna. Be with us this night.
All	Be with us this night.
Priestess	The cold weather keeps us indoors at this time of year and helps us focus inward. The spiral of energy that we followed at Yule continues to draw us to our center to face that which we truly are.

To aid us on our inward journey we are going to do a winter meditation. At this time of year the elements are harsh, yet they have their own special beauty and purpose. Take a few minutes to relax. Close your eyes and let go of the day. Let go of everyday thoughts, everyday cares. Breathe slowly, deeply, evenly. Feel your energy settle and come to center.

Background

Read the guided meditation.

Priestess	Take time to feel yourself fully back in your body, fully back in this time.

Closing

After speaking, each participant extinguishes the candle he or she lit at the beginning of the ritual.

Priestess	Lady of Darkness, of energy that moves us with the rhythm of the moon, we thank you for your presence and guidance. Stay if you will; go if you must. Hail and farewell.
All	Hail and farewell. Blessed be.
Priest	Lord of Winter, white warrior of snow and winter winds, we thank you for your presence and teachings. Stay if you will; go if you must. Hail and farewell.
All	Hail and farewell. Blessed be.
West	Spirits of the west, of frozen water that sparkles like precious crystal, we thank you for your presence this night. Stay if you will; go if you must. Hail and farewell.

All	Hail and farewell. Blessed be.
South	Spirits of the south, of fire that keeps the icy chill from our bones, we thank you for your presence this night. Stay if you will; go if you must. Hail and farewell.
All	Hail and farewell. Blessed be.
East	Spirits of the east, of air that catches our breath in wintry wisps, we thank you for your presence this night. Stay if you will; go if you must. Hail and farewell.
All	Hail and farewell. Blessed be.
North	Spirits of the north, of earth that sleeps until spring calls, we thank you for your presence this night. Stay if you will; go if you must. Hail and farewell.
All	Hail and farewell. Blessed be.

Everyone joins hands around the circle.

Priestess	Our first circle of the year will be open but unbroken. May its energy sustain us through our winter's journey.
All	Merry meet, merry part, and merry meet again. Blessed be.

Solo Ritual

Casting the Circle

With your athame or wand, walk the perimeter of your circle, saying:

> The night is dark, the world is still,
> Seeds rest beneath snow-covered hills.
> Waiting for spring, I turn within,
> To other realms, 'tis time to begin.
> I create sacred space with this first circle of the year.

Calling the Quarters

Walk to the edge of the circle in each direction respectively as you speak, and then light a candle on the altar. Stand in front of the altar to evoke the Goddess and God.

Speak   Hail, spirits of north, of earth wrapped in slumber. Below the snow and ice you rest and wait for the time of awakening. Be with me this night.

Hail, spirits of east, of air shrouded with winter fog. Your blanket of white brings a quiet stillness to the world. Be with me this night.

Hail, spirits of south, of fire warm and inviting. Keep alive the spark of life that sleeps within Mother Gaia. Be with me this night.

Hail, spirits of west, of water suspended like diamonds in winter's icy hand. Hold your secrets until you flow again. Be with me this night.

Hail, Lord of Winter, harsh and challenging. Your driving storms bring both beauty and danger. Your lessons I must learn. Be with me this night.

Hail, Lady of Darkness, of star-studded heavens. Your crisp cold nights vibrate with the silvery gift of Luna. Be with me this night.

Make yourself comfortable to listen to the tape. You may want to use headphones to block out any unwanted noises that might distract your meditation.

Closing

Stand in front of the altar when addressing the Goddess and God. Walk to the edge of the circle in the respective direction as you dismiss each. After speaking, extinguish a candle on the altar.

Speak   Lady of Darkness, of energy that moves me with the rhythm of the moon, thank you for your presence and guidance. Stay if you will; go if you must. Hail and farewell.

Lord of Winter, white warrior of snow and winter winds, thank you for your presence and teachings. Stay if you will; go if you must. Hail and farewell.

Spirits of the west, of frozen water that sparkles like precious crystal, thank you for your presence this night. Stay if you will; go if you must. Hail and farewell.

Spirits of the south, of fire that keeps the icy chill from my bones, thank you for your presence this night. Stay if you will; go if you must. Hail and farewell.

Spirits of the east, of air that catches my breath in wintry wisps, thank you for your presence this night. Stay if you will; go if you must. Hail and farewell.

Spirits of the north, of earth that sleeps until spring calls, thank you for your presence this night. Stay if you will; go if you must. Hail and farewell.

> The first circle of the year is open,
> But like the web of life, unbroken.
> Through the winter may it sustain me,
> In faith and unity, blessed be.

MOON OF THE SEER

february

The night of the year is drawing to a close, but just as a storm can be most fierce before it ends, winter can be most brutal just before spring. In February we continue to work with our inner power and confront our personal truths. The full moon of this month sheds enough light for us to see into our own darkness.

Other Names for This Moon

- Storm Moon

- Snow Moon

- Quickening Moon

In the Celtic Tree Calendar

February 1–17: Rowan—associated with the coming of new life born from the dark of winter, protection, and strength; the goddess Brigid.

February 18–29: Ash—associated with the sea (myths tell of it having come from the undersea realm of Tethys), protection; the god Manannan.

Background for This Ritual

Solo practitioners will want to read this just before beginning the ritual. A place has been indicated in the group ritual where this is most appropriate for the Priestess or Priest to read to everyone:

The growing light gives us hope, but there are still hard days of winter ahead. Even with the icy grip still upon the world, you feel the lifeforce awakening and know that your life must begin to quicken. Many things can unfold this year, but which way should you go?

The sabbat of Imbolg and the month of February are times for divination. This is the time of the "seer" within.

This month is touched by the rowan and ash. The rowan tree brings magic and the protection of Brigid. As the goddess who governs crossroads, Brigid can see all possible paths for the traveler.

The ash tree is also associated with divination. It was upon the ash that Odin suspended himself and from which he perceived the runes. This is why ash is frequently used as rune tiles. In times past, the wood of the ash tree was used for divination fires where one would scry the flames for images and signs. Finding an ash leaf with an equal number of sections on either side of the center vein is considered a sign of good luck.

In addition to the runes, another form of divination associated with trees is the ancient Celtic ogham alphabet, also known simply as the tree alphabet. Each letter is named for a particular tree. Each tree has certain aspects and attributes that can be related to your personal life. In the ritual, you will select one of the cards from the deck of tree cards.

If a message is not immediately clear to you, don't try to force something to happen. Simply note any sensations you may experience or images that may come into your mind. Messages from other realms are not always quickly revealed. An image or thought may need to settle for a day or two, perhaps longer. Don't rush. The information will come to you when you are ready for it.

Themes

- Use a method of divination to discern your path in the coming months.

- Strengthen your connection with the natural world through ogham divination.

Preparation

Items needed for this ritual include the following:

- Six candles

- Cauldron made of cast iron or other metal in which you can safely burn things

- A stick inscribed with the Celtic ogham tree alphabet (see appendix B for the ogham)

- Celtic tree cards (see appendix B)

- Pencils and small pieces of paper, enough for each participant

- A set of runes to decorate the altar (optional)

FOR SOLO RITUAL

- Taped meditative music (optional)

- Wand or athame (optional)

Group Ritual

Priestess   The skies are gray and the weather is still cold, but the snow is receding. Underneath the ground life starts to secretly stir with the promise of rebirth. As the days grow steadily longer we can feel our souls begin to awaken.

Casting the Circle

The Priestess holds a stick inscribed with the ogham Celtic tree alphabet.

Priestess   Our names carry power that we share with one another. Tonight we cast our circle by naming ourselves. I am _____.

After stating her name, the Priestess passes the stick to the person on her left. Deosil around the circle, each person states his or her name and passes the stick. When it is returned to the Priestess, she says:

By the powers of Odin and Brigid, the circle is cast. We have created and become sacred space.

Calling the Quarters

Each participant faces his or her direction while speaking, and then lights a candle on the altar. The Priest and Priestess stand in front of the altar to evoke deity.

North	Come ye spirits of north, of earth our foundation. Hidden in your belly are the secrets of what will be. You know where all seeds lie and wait to be sent forth. We bid you welcome.
All	We bid you welcome.
East	Come ye spirits of east, of air cold and invigorating. Your icy blasts keep us in the grip of winter, yet you bring a hint of milder times to come. We bid you welcome.
All	We bid you welcome.
South	Come ye spirits of south, of fire our beacon through the dark of the year. Warm the earth and entice plants to part the snow. We bid you welcome.
All	We bid you welcome.
West	Come ye spirits of west, of water that feeds all life. Flow once again in swift, clear streams. We bid you welcome.
All	We bid you welcome.
Priest	Come ye Lord Odin. In your sacrifice you found answers. Help us divine what is hidden within. We bid you welcome.
All	We bid you welcome.
Priestess	Come ye Brigid, lady who knows all things. As we stand at the crossroads of the year, help us discern our path ahead. We bid you welcome.
All	We bid you welcome.

Background

Share the background information here.

The Priestess passes around the pencils and paper. Holding up the deck of tree cards, the Priest says:

> As I come around the circle, each person will have an opportunity to draw a card. With the pencil and paper given to you, note the name of the tree

and its aspects. Then soften your gaze as you look at the tree name. Ponder its attributes and how they may relate to your life.

You will be drawn to choose a particular card because it has information for you. Something of that tree's attributes is important in the coming year. It will tell you something about the path you are to follow or what it is you need to look for in yourself. Perhaps there is an aspect of yourself that is ready to be cultivated. Take time to explore the message. Open your heart and mind to receive.

Raising the ogham stick, the Priestess says:

Odin, Brigid, we call on your powers to see the many roads ahead. Reveal to us our individual paths. May we be blessed with the insight to read your signs.

When everyone has drawn a card, the Priestess and Priest may want to softly and slowly drum, chant, or hum as participants meditate on the information.

Priestess   After you have settled on the message you are to receive and pondered its meaning, commit the information to memory. When you are ready, come to the altar, pass the paper upon which you have written the tree name through the candle flame, and then cast it into the cauldron. The cauldron is a symbol of transformation. As you watch the paper burn, think of how the attributes will transform and manifest into your life. These ashes will be committed to the earth after our ritual has ended.

As participants burn their papers, the Priestess and Priest once more chant, drum, or hum. Others may join in. When everyone has burned their paper, the Priestess says:

Odin, Brigid, we thank you for your guidance this night. May we be touched by your blessings. As above, so below. Blessed be.

All   Blessed be.

Priest   You may want to sit on the floor or put your hands on the floor. Close your eyes. Take time to let your energy flow down through your body, down through you and into the earth. Touch your energy to Mother Earth. Feel her balance bring you to center. When you are ready, open your eyes.

Closing

Once again, each participant faces his or her respective direction while speaking, and then extinguishes his or her candle. The Priest and Priestess face the altar as they speak.

Priestess Brigid, Lady of the Crossroads, we thank you for your presence in our circle this night. May we be blessed with your wisdom and guided by your love. Ere you depart to your realm, we bid you farewell.

All We bid you farewell. Blessed be.

Priest Odin, Lord of Divination, we thank you for your presence in our circle this night. May we be blessed with your great knowledge and guided by your courage. Ere you depart to your realm, we bid you farewell.

All We bid you farewell. Blessed be.

West Spirits of west, of the watery realm, we thank you for your presence in our circle this night. May we be blessed with the ability to flow with life's currents. Ere you depart to your realm, we bid you farewell.

All We bid you farewell. Blessed be.

South Spirits of south, of the fiery realm, we thank you for your presence in our circle this night. May we be blessed with the ability to find the beacon that illuminates the way ahead. Ere you depart to your realm, we bid you farewell.

All We bid you farewell. Blessed be.

East Spirits of east, of the airy realm, we thank you for your presence in our circle this night. May we be blessed with the ability to rise above difficulties that may challenge us. Ere you depart to your realm, we bid you farewell.

All We bid you farewell. Blessed be.

North Spirits of north, of the earthly realm, we thank you for your presence in our circle this night. May we be blessed with the ability to remain centered and strong. Ere you depart to your realm, we bid you farewell.

All We bid you farewell. Blessed be.

Priestess Our night of divination has come to an end, but the messages given us and the paths we are to tread will continue to unfold. The blessed ones will guide us until next we gather.

All Merry meet, merry part, and merry meet again.

The Priest and Priestess may want to invite participants to join them in burying the ashes in the earth.

Solo Ritual

Casting the Circle

Using a stick inscribed with the ogham alphabet, begin walking around the perimeter of your circle as you say:

> Cold wind, skies gray,
> Light grows each day.
> Life stirs secretly,
> Soul awakens in me.
> By the powers of Odin and Brigid,
> sacred is this space decreed.

Calling the Quarters

Walk to the edge of the circle in the respective direction as you call each. After speaking, light a candle on the altar. Stand in front of the altar to evoke the Goddess and God.

Speak Come ye spirits of north, of earth my foundation. Hidden in your belly are the secrets of what will be. You know where all seeds lie and wait to be sent forth. I bid you welcome.

Come ye spirits of east, of air cold and invigorating. Your icy blasts keep the world in the grip of winter, yet you bring a hint of milder times to come. I bid you welcome.

Come ye spirits of south, of fire my beacon through the dark of the year. Warm the earth and entice plants to part the snow. I bid you welcome.

Come ye spirits of west, of water that feeds all life. Flow once again in swift, clear streams. I bid you welcome.

Come ye Lord Odin. In your sacrifice you found answers. Help me divine what is hidden within. I bid you welcome.

Come ye Brigid, lady who knows all things. As I stand at the crossroads of the year, help me discern my path ahead. I bid you welcome.

Hold the deck of tree cards. Choose a card, and then say:

Odin, Brigid, I call on your powers to see the many roads ahead. Reveal to me my path. May I be blessed with the insight to read your signs.

Write the tree name and attributes on a separate piece of paper. Soften your gaze as you look at the tree name. Ponder its attributes and how they may relate to your life. Use taped music for your meditation if you choose.

After the message of the card is clear to you, commit the information to memory. When you are ready, pass the paper upon which you have written the tree name through the candle flame, and then cast it into the cauldron. As you watch the paper burn, think of how the attributes will transform and manifest into your life.

After your paper has burned, say:

Odin, Brigid, I thank you for your guidance this night. May I be touched by your blessings. As above, so below. Blessed be.

Use your usual method for grounding energy.

Closing

Walk to the edge of the circle in the respective direction as you dismiss each. After speaking, extinguish a candle on the altar. Stand in front of the altar to address the Goddess and God.

Speak   Brigid, Lady of the Crossroads, thank you for your presence in my circle this night. May I be blessed with your wisdom and guided by your love. Ere you depart to your realm, I bid you farewell.

Odin, Lord of Divination, thank you for your presence in my circle this night. May I be blessed with your great knowledge and guided by your courage. Ere you depart to your realm, I bid you farewell.

Spirits of west, of the watery realm, thank you for your presence in my circle this night. May I be blessed with the ability to flow with life's currents. Ere you depart to your realm, I bid you farewell.

Spirits of south, of the fiery realm, thank you for your presence in my circle this night. May I be blessed with the ability to find the beacon that illuminates the way ahead. Ere you depart to your realm, I bid you farewell.

Spirits of east, of the airy realm, thank you for your presence in my circle this night. May I be blessed with the ability to rise above difficulties that may challenge me. Ere you depart to your realm, I bid you farewell.

Spirits of north, of the earthly realm, thank you for your presence in my circle this night. May I be blessed with the ability to remain centered and strong. Ere you depart to your realm, I bid you farewell.

> My circle is open but unbroken,
> No longer sacred this space I decree.
> May the blessed ones guide my path,
> In faith and unity, blessed be.

Take the ashes from the cauldron and bury them in the earth.

MOON OF THE WIND

March

The earth awakens as the bonds of winter loosen. This windy month blows away the staleness of winter and with it we cast away the things we need to remove from our lives. Holding on to things that no longer belong in our lives can keep us from moving forward. Just as our homes need a spring-cleaning, so, too, do our emotional and spiritual lives.

Other Names for This Moon

- Quickening Moon
- Wind Moon
- Hare Moon

In the Celtic Tree Calendar

March 1–17: Ash—in addition to being associated with the sea, ash also has connections with the runes and besom brooms.

March 18–31: Alder—associated with courage, strength, and evolving one's spirit; Celtic hero Bran.

Background for This Ritual

A place has been indicated in the group ritual where this is most appropriate for the Priestess or Priest to read both Parts I and II to everyone. Solo practitioners will want to read Part I before beginning the ritual and Part II where indicated:

Part I: March is a time to make ready for spring. Waters run freely from snowmelt, and bright yellow daffodils beckon the sun's warmth. Nights are still tinged with frost, but it is time to begin preparations for spring, time to clear away winter's rubble from the garden and from your life—both physical and spiritual.

The ash, which is a tree for part of this month, is one of the traditional materials for a besom broom along with birch and willow. Besoms are used frequently in fertility rituals and handfasting ceremonies. Associated with the element water, they not only sweep physical dirt from an area that is to be made sacred, but also psychic dirt and negative energy. Alder, the other tree of March, provides strength and courage to clear away things from your life and to start fresh.

In this time of clearing away and making ready for spring, use your besom to symbolically remove negativity from your life. Action begins with intention: tonight send the intention to clear out anything that may be holding you back or preventing you from growing in some way.

Part II: Hold your broom in front of you with both hands, handle pointing up. Raise it so your hands are at chest level and the brush is resting gently on the floor.

Close your eyes and draw earth energy up through your body and through the broom. Feel it come up through your spine to your heart center and through the besom, along your arms to your heart. Feel this strong connection of your energy, Mother Earth's energy, and the spirit of the besom. Feel this combine into one smooth flow.

Give thought to what you need to remove and clear away from your life. Spring is almost here and it is time to make ready for new spiritual growth. Just as you clear a garden for the new season, so, too, must you clear your soul and psyche. When you have fixed your mind on the things that need removal, open your eyes.

Themes

- Cast out unneeded things from our lives (spring-cleaning).

- Make room for new growth and new things to enter our lives.

Preparation

Items needed for this ritual include the following:

- A besom broom or a bundle of twigs, straw, or heather for each participant

- Six gemstones or crystals to use in place of candles for the altar, one in each color for directions/elements according to your tradition (see Table 2 in appendix A)

- Two white quartz or purple amethyst for the Goddess and God

Group Ritual

Priestess   Life is stirring and beginning to burst forth from the womb of the earth. The world is rousing into motion after a winter's slumber. It is time to awaken our hearts to this quickening rhythm.

Casting the Circle

Priestess   From one to the other our circle is cast.

The Priestess places her left hand on the shoulder of the person next to her. With her right hand, she raises the brush end of her besom broom toward the altar. Each person repeats the phrase around the circle, following suit until a connection is made around the room and all brooms are raised.

Priestess   By the magic of these besoms we have created sacred space.

Calling the Quarters

Each participant doing an evocation should have his or her gemstone or crystal before the ritual starts. After speaking, he or she places it on the altar.

North	Spirits of earth, we beckon ye from the north. You have sustained us through the winter. We now ask that you help us stretch and grow. Join us under Luna's watchful gaze.
All	Join us under Luna's watchful gaze.
East	Spirits of air, we beckon ye from the east. With your mighty winds of March we ask that you blow away the staleness of winter. Join us under Luna's watchful gaze.
All	Join us under Luna's watchful gaze.
South	Spirits of fire, we beckon ye from the south. We ask that you purify our hearts and lives as we clear away the remnants of winter. Join us under Luna's watchful gaze.
All	Join us under Luna's watchful gaze.
West	Spirits of water, we beckon ye from the west. We ask that you bathe us in your cleansing streams as we prepare for the months ahead. Join us under Luna's watchful gaze.
All	Join us under Luna's watchful gaze.
Priest	We beckon ye Dagda, Great Lord of All. As spring gains a firm foothold we ask that you help us prepare our path ahead through the coming months. Join us under Luna's watchful gaze.
All	Join us under Luna's watchful gaze.
Priestess	We beckon ye Dana, Great Lady of All. As the warmth of spring approaches we ask that you help us open our hearts to receive your guidance. Join us under Luna's watchful gaze.
All	Join us under Luna's watchful gaze.

Background

Share Parts I and II of the background information here.

| Priest | Move in close to the center of our circle and raise your besom so that we touch the brushes of our brooms above the altar. Send energy to the center of our besom circle. Feel it build and add strength to each of us. |

Now draw your besom up from the circle, over your head in an arch, and down to the floor. Sweep along the floor from the center and out to the edge of our circle. With each motion visualize that you are casting out that which you wish to be rid of. Each smooth long motion lightens your life. Once you reach the edge of the circle you may want to lift the broom and dance in place. Once everyone has reached the edge we will move deosil around the circle to share strength in casting away unwanted things. As we do this we also strengthen our circle and connection with one another.

The Priestess begins the chant:

Besom broom of power and light,
Cast out darkness; set to flight
Things unwanted that hinder me,
This is my will; so mote it be.

After circling around the altar a few times, the Priest and Priestess slow the chant and bring the movement to a halt.

| Priestess | It is time to move back into the everyday realm. You may want to sit on the floor or put your hands on the floor. Close your eyes for a moment. Take time to let your energy flow down through your body. Down through you and into the earth. Touch your energy to Mother Earth. Feel her balance bring you to center. When you are ready, open your eyes. |

Closing

Each participant faces his or her respective direction while speaking. The Priest and Priestess stand in front of the altar. The stones or crystals placed on the altar can remain there.

| Priestess | Dana, Great Lady of All, thank you for your guidance in removing that which is unwanted and unneeded from our lives. Thank you for your presence in our circle this night. Stay if you will; go if you must. We bid thee farewell. |

| All | We bid thee farewell. Blessed be. |

Priest Dagda, Great Lord of All, thank you for your help in sweeping away negative energy from our lives. Thank you for your presence in our circle this night. Stay if you will; go if you must. We bid thee farewell.

All We bid thee farewell. Blessed be.

West Spirits of west, of water, thank you for washing away that which is unneeded in our lives. Thank you for your presence in our circle this night. Stay if you will; go if you must. We bid thee farewell.

All We bid thee farewell. Blessed be.

South Spirits of south, of fire, thank you for burning away that which is unwanted in our lives. Thank you for your presence in our circle this night. Stay if you will; go if you must. We bid thee farewell.

All We bid thee farewell. Blessed be.

East Spirits of east, of air, thank you for blowing away that which is unneeded in our lives. Thank you for your presence in our circle this night. Stay if you will; go if you must. We bid thee farewell.

All We bid thee farewell. Blessed be.

North Spirits of north, of earth, thank you for removing that which is unwanted in our lives. Thank you for your presence in our circle this night. Stay if you will; go if you must. We bid thee farewell.

All We bid thee farewell. Blessed be.

Everyone joins hands around the circle with their besoms held in their left. Let the broom end of the besoms rest on the floor.

Priestess

Star light, star bright,

It is time to take flight.

Besom sturdy held upright,

Off we go through dark of night.

Blessed be.

All Merry meet, merry part, and merry meet again.

Solo Ritual

Casting the Circle

With your broom touching the floor, walk around the perimeter of your circle while saying:

> In the earth life is stirring,
> Winter's gone, now awake,
> To the rhythm of the quickening,
> Bring life forth and magic make.

When you return to where you started, say:
> By the magic of this besom, sacred is this space decreed.

Calling the Quarters

After speaking, place the gemstone or crystal on the altar for each respective direction and deity.

Speak   Spirits of earth, I beckon ye from the north. You have sustained me through the winter. I now ask that you help me stretch and grow. Join me under Luna's watchful gaze.

Spirits of air, I beckon ye from the east. With your mighty winds of March I ask that you blow away the staleness of winter. Join me under Luna's watchful gaze.

Spirits of fire, I beckon ye from the south. Purify my heart and life as I clear away the remnants of winter. Join me under Luna's watchful gaze.

Spirits of water, I beckon ye from the west. Bathe me in your cleansing streams as I prepare for the months ahead. Join me under Luna's watchful gaze.

I beckon ye Dagda, Great Lord of All. As spring gains a firm foothold I ask that you help me prepare my path ahead through the coming months. Join me under Luna's watchful gaze.

I beckon ye Dana, Great Lady of All. As the warmth of spring approaches I ask that you help me open my heart to receive your guidance. Join me under Luna's watchful gaze.

Background

Read Part II of the information and continue:

Move to the center of your circle and raise the besom above the altar. Walk around the altar with your broom raised above it. When you get back to where you started, draw your besom up over your head in an arch, and down to the floor. Sweep along the floor from the center and out to the edge of your circle. With each motion visualize that you are casting out the things you want to remove from your life. Once you reach the edge of the circle, begin sweeping around the perimeter as you chant:

<blockquote>
Besom broom of power and light,
Cast out darkness; set to flight
Things unwanted that hinder me,
This is my will; so mote it be.
</blockquote>

When it feels appropriate, bring the chant and movement to a halt. Use your usual method for grounding energy.

Closing

Face each direction, respectively, while speaking. Face the altar for the Goddess and God. The stones or crystals placed on the altar can remain there.

Speak   Dana, Great Lady of All, thank you for your guidance in removing that which is unwanted and unneeded from my life. Thank you for your presence in my circle this night. Stay if you will; go if you must. I bid thee farewell.

Dagda, Great Lord of All, thank you for your help in sweeping away negative energy from my life. Thank you for your presence in my circle this night. Stay if you will; go if you must. I bid thee farewell.

Spirits of west, of water, thank you for washing away that which is unneeded in my life. Thank you for your presence in my circle this night. Stay if you will; go if you must. I bid thee farewell.

Spirits of south, of fire, thank you for burning away that which is unwanted in my life. Thank you for your presence in my circle this night. Stay if you will; go if you must. I bid thee farewell.

Spirits of east, of air, thank you for blowing away that which is unneeded in my life. Thank you for your presence in my circle this night. Stay if you will; go if you must. I bid thee farewell.

Spirits of north, of earth, thank you for removing that which is unwanted in my life. Thank you for your presence in my circle this night. Stay if you will; go if you must. I bid thee farewell.

Star light, star bright,
It is time to take flight.
Besom sturdy held upright,
Off I go through dark of night.
Blessed be.

MOON OF THE WATERS

April

Life is bursting forth with renewed vigor, and the earth is turning many shades of lush green. Each rain shower seems to bring more plants and trees to life. In the moonlight the softness of spring becomes a shimmering pool of lifeforce energy that feeds our bodies and souls.

Other Names for This Moon

- Seed Moon

- Grass Moon

- Rain Moon

In the Celtic Tree Calendar

April 1–14: Alder—associated with courage, strength, and evolving one's spirit; Celtic hero Bran.

April 15–30: Willow—associated with enchantment and death; willow trees are usually found growing near water; Celtic goddesses Danu and Morigan.

Background for This Ritual

A place has been indicated in both the group and solo rituals where it is appropriate to read this:

Water, *fons et origo*—the source of all possible existence. It provides outward purification and serves to symbolically purify us within. Springs and wells are considered holy because of the power of spirit that resides there. They also serve as gateways between the worlds and are places to commune with the Divine. Like its opposite element, fire, water has the diametric powers to destroy or heal.

In the ancient Goddess-worshipping cultures, the Goddess was portrayed as both woman and waterbird and many of her symbols were aquatic. This mothering, life-giving aspect was not only connected with giving birth, but also encompassed life-sustaining, nurturing, and protective aspects of her being.

In our overbearing society it is important to emphasize and honor our abilities to nurture. It is equally important for men to do this. Tonight's ritual is intended to help you acknowledge yourself as a creator and nurturer.

As you pour a little water from the pitcher into this large bowl, state a nurturing affirmation about yourself. It could be that you are raising a child, tending a garden, or you do something artistic or musical, not necessarily as a profession. You could be caring for an elderly parent, teaching a class, or simply picking up trash when you go for a walk.

Themes

- Acknowledge the importance of water.

- Celebrate your nurturing qualities.

- Honor the flowing and changing of life energy.

Preparation

Items needed for this ritual include:

- Small bowl of water

- Empty large bowl for group ritual, or small one for solo ritual

- Empty large pitcher for group ritual, or small one for solo ritual

- One cut flower

- Four candles for the altar for the directions (use colors that are appropriate for your tradition or refer to Table 2 in appendix A)

- Two candles of the color of your choice for the Goddess and God

Also, participants should be instructed to bring a small jar of water from a favorite place where they like to walk or where they have vacationed. If water cannot be collected from a particular place, instruct participants as follows: Pour a small cup of pure spring water, and then hold it between your hands. Close your eyes and visualize a place where you have been. Let your joy and remembrance of this place become part of the water you hold.

OPTIONAL
- Drums and other percussion instruments

- A tape/CD of a waterfall, bubbling stream, or trickling fountain

FOR SOLO RITUAL
Gather water from several places or do separate visualizations to have water represent different sources you have visited. Before starting your ritual, place the jars of water at various points on the perimeter of your circle.

Group Ritual

Priestess   *Tempus vernum*—springtime. This is a month of dewy mornings and frequent showers that coax the flowers from the bosom of Mother Earth. Leaves are coming on to the trees, and the world is nourished by heavenly rains.

Casting the Circle

Taking a flower from the altar and a small bowl of water, the Priestess dips the flower into the water and sprinkles the ground as she walks around the circle. When finished, she says:

From water we are born, with water we are nourished. We create a pool of sacred space with this precious element.

Calling the Quarters

Each participant faces his or her respective direction while speaking (the Priest and Priestess face the altar), and then lights a candle.

North	*Septentrio:* We call to the north, realm of earth. You are our foundation on this planet of great oceans. Your color, brown, represents the sustenance of the Goddess. Be here this night to celebrate. We bid you welcome.
All	We bid you welcome.
East	*Oriens:* We call to the east, realm of air. You deliver rains to us in gentle showers and stormy torrents. Your color, light blue, represents the nurturing breath of the Goddess. Be here this night to celebrate. We bid you welcome.
All	We bid you welcome.
South	*Meridians:* We call to the south, realm of fire. Your heat warms the water that flows across the world. Your color, red, represents the life-giving blood of the Goddess. Be here this night to celebrate. We bid you welcome.
All	We bid you welcome.
West	*Occidens:* We call to the west, realm of water. Your gift feeds us, soothes us, and washes us clean. Your color, dark blue, represents the protection of the Goddess. Be here this night to celebrate. We bid you welcome.
All	We bid you welcome.
Priest	We call to the Lord, Manannan, Neptune, Poseidon. May the mysteries of your watery realm bring magic and strength to our circle. Be here this night to celebrate. We bid you welcome.
All	We bid you welcome.
Priestess	We call to the Lady Brigid, Boann, Aphrodite. The moisture of your womb gives life to the world, and your holy wells provide sustenance and solace. Be here this night to celebrate. We bid you welcome.

All   We bid you welcome.

Priestess   The meadows are greening and trees are bursting into leaf. At this time of year brilliant sunny mornings can give way to blustery, rainy afternoons. Water is important in this season to nourish the things that are only beginning to grow.

Priest   Tonight we bring together water from many sources for our celebration.

The Priest takes a large pitcher from the altar and walks deosil around the circle, pausing for each participant to pour water into it. After he completes the circuit, he faces the Priestess and holds the pitcher forward for her to also grasp. Together they say:

Lord and Lady, we ask for your blessings on this water we have collected. May it hold power for our ritual this night.

All   So mote it be.

Background

Share the background information here.

After everyone has made an affirmation:

Priest   Singing and chanting is a way to honor deity and ourselves. It also puts more energy into our intentions as we send them out to the universe. Tonight, let the universe know that we think it's important to be nurturers as we chant:

> Listen to the voice,
> The voice of the water,
> The voice of the Mother,
> Calling you and me.

In addition to chanting, participants may choose to drum and/or dance. When it seems appropriate, the Priestess will bring the chanting and drumming to a stop. Before speaking, she pours the water from the bowl back into the pitcher, and says:

Close your eyes and let your energy unwind.

Slowly, she pours the water back into the bowl, saying:

> Listen to the water as it trickles down toward the earth. Let your energy follow it. Down, down to join the Mother in her sacred pool. Let your energy touch the earth and the water. Let it bring you to center. When you feel balanced, open your eyes.

Closing

In turn, each participant who lit a candle extinguishes it after speaking.

Priestess Lady of Water, Brigid, Boann, Aphrodite, thank you for giving us life and for bestowing life on this beautiful world. Thank you for your presence in our circle this night. Stay if you will; go if you must. We bid you farewell.

All We bid you farewell. Blessed be.

Priest Lord of Water, Manannan, Nepture, Poseidon, thank you for the magic that your watery realm provides. Thank you for your presence in our circle this night. Stay if you will; go if you must. We bid you farewell.

All We bid you farewell. Blessed be.

West Powers of west, of water, thank you for your sacred gift and for your presence in our circle this night. Stay if you will; go if you must. We bid you farewell.

All We bid you farewell. Blessed be.

South Powers of south, of fire, thank you for the heat that warms the rains and for your presence in our circle this night. Stay if you will; go if you must. We bid you farewell.

All We bid you farewell. Blessed be.

East Powers of east, of air, thank you for bringing the rains and for your presence in our circle this night. Stay if you will; go if you must. We bid you farewell.

All We bid you farewell. Blessed be.

North	Powers of north, of earth, thank you for supporting the great rivers and oceans and for your presence in our circle this night. Stay if you will; go if you must. We bid you farewell.
All	We bid you farewell. Blessed be.

Everyone joins hands around the circle.

Priestess	To be in sacred space is to be in the river of life. It is to know that life is energy and that everything flows and changes. May we continue to seek and affirm the nurturing and sustaining aspects in ourselves and those around us. Our pool of sacred space will be open but unbroken, and its loving energy will remain in our hearts.
All	Merry meet, merry part, and merry meet again.

Solo Ritual

Casting the Circle

Take the small bowl of water and flower from the altar. Dip the flower into the water and sprinkle the ground as you walk around the circle saying:

Tempus vernum, springtime brings
Dewy mornings and gentle showers,
Trees in leaf and fragrant flowers.

When you return to your starting point, say:

From water I am born, with water I am nourished. Tonight I create a pool of sacred space with this precious element.

Calling the Quarters

Face each direction as you speak and then light the respective candle. For the Goddess and God, stand facing the altar.

Speak	*Septentrio:* I call to the north, realm of earth. You are my foundation on this planet of great oceans. Your color, brown, represents the sustenance of the Goddess. Be here this night to celebrate. I bid you welcome.

Oriens: I call to the east, realm of air. You deliver rain in gentle showers and stormy torrents. Your color, light blue, represents the nurturing breath of the Goddess. Be here this night to celebrate. I bid you welcome.

Meridians: I call to the south, realm of fire. Your heat warms the water that flows across the world. Your color, red, represents the life-giving blood of the Goddess. Be here this night to celebrate. I bid you welcome.

Occidens: I call to the west, realm of water. Your gift feeds me, soothes me, and washes me clean. Your color, dark blue, represents the protection of the Goddess. Be here this night to celebrate. I bid you welcome.

I call to the Lord, Manannan, Neptune, Poseidon. May the mysteries of your watery realm bring magic and strength to my circle. Be here this night to celebrate. I bid you welcome.

I call to the Lady Brigid, Boann, Aphrodite. The moisture of your womb gives life to the world, and your holy wells provide sustenance and solace. Be here this night to celebrate. I bid you welcome.

Tonight I bring together water from various sources for my celebration.

Take the pitcher from the altar and walk deosil around the circle. As you come to each jar of water, pour its contents into the pitcher. After you complete the circuit, face the altar and say:

Lord and Lady, I ask for your blessings on this water. May it hold power for my ritual this night.

Background

Read the background information here.

Singing and chanting is a way to honor deity and yourself. It also adds energy to your intentions as you send them out to the universe. Let the universe know that you think it's okay to be a nurturing person. You may also want to drum as you chant:

Listen to the voice,
The voice of the water,
The voice of the Mother,
Calling you and me.

When it feels appropriate, bring the chanting and drumming to a stop. If you have a water-fall/bubbling brook tape or CD, play it as you use your usual method of grounding energy.

Closing

After speaking each part, extinguish the appropriate altar candle.

Speak   Lady of Water, Brigid, Boann, Aphrodite, thank you for the gift of life and for bestowing life on this beautiful world. Thank you for your presence in my circle this night. Stay if you will; go if you must. I bid you farewell.

Lord of Water, Manannan, Nepture, Poseidon, thank you for the magic that your watery realm provides. Thank you for your presence in my circle this night. Stay if you will; go if you must. I bid you farewell.

Powers of west, of water, thank you for your sacred gift and for your presence in my circle this night. Stay if you will; go if you must. I bid you farewell.

Powers of south, of fire, thank you for the heat that warms the water and for your presence in my circle this night. Stay if you will; go if you must. I bid you farewell.

Powers of east, of air, thank you for bringing the rains and for your presence in my circle this night. Stay if you will; go if you must. I bid you farewell.

Powers of north, of earth, thank you for supporting the great rivers and oceans and for your presence in my circle this night. Stay if you will; go if you must. I bid you farewell.

Walk the perimeter of your circle as you say:

> River of life knows
> Nurturing love flows
> From deep inside me
> With faith, blessed be.

MOON OF THE FAERIES

May

It is no surprise that May is called the magical month. The world seems transformed into a beautiful garden awash in color as flowers and fruit trees bloom and fill the air with a potpourri of sweet perfume. Under the moonlight it is easy to feel the enchantment of the other realms. Open your heart and let your energy reach out.

Other Names for This Moon

- Flower Moon

- Milk Moon

- Merry Moon

In the Celtic Tree Calendar

May 1–12: Willow—associated with flexibility, the power of intuition, and the inner voice; gaining balance, healing, death.

May 13–31: Hawthorne—associated with healing and balance, spiritual energies, protection, hope, pleasure, the faeries.

Background for This Ritual

Places have been indicated in both the solo and group rituals where Parts I and II should be read:

Part I: This is May, the time of opening, the time of blossoming. The world is gently wrapped in a sweet blanket of flowers. Fruit trees bloom and carry the promise of abundance to come. Newly arrived birds sing in the warmth of the strengthening sunlight. We do ritual in this soft part of the year to open our spirits to receive.

Flowers, a gift from the Lord and Lady, beckon to our souls. Their endless varieties give us beauty and fragrance to enjoy. Some flowers, such as lavender, can be used for healing and others, such as geraniums, can be used to enhance the flavor of food.

Like flowers, we are children of Mother Earth, and in this time of blossoming, we, too, need to open. Flowers are delicate and beautiful and serve to remind us that we need to be gentle with ourselves and to be able to find the beauty within.

Marigold seeds are used in this ritual. For centuries it was believed that to smell or gaze upon a marigold would lift cares and burdens from your soul. Tonight we use the gift of marigold to lift the cares of everyday life from our shoulders and to help open our hearts.

Cup the seeds in your hands and hold them near your heart. Close your eyes and think of how you want to blossom. Think of how you want to open and receive the good things that are waiting to come into your life. Think of your spirit opening like a flower. Let it bloom.

Part II: When you have fixed that image in your mind, go to the altar and place the seeds in the cauldron. The cauldron is an ancient symbol of the womb and of transformation. After you have placed the seeds in the cauldron, take a flower from the basket. Receive it as a precious gift.

Themes

- Employ the symbolic meaning of flowers to aid your intentions.

- Acknowledge the gentleness of your spirit.

Preparation

Items needed for this ritual include the following:

- Two cut flowers provided by each participant

- A basket to hold the flowers

- A separate basket containing enough cut flowers to give one to each participant and a few extras for participants who may not have brought their own

- Six candles in pastel or early spring flower colors

- A small cauldron

- A bowl filled with enough marigold seeds to give a pinch to each participant

- Enough sachets containing morning glory and moon flower seeds to give one to each participant (see instructions in appendix D)

For Solo Ritual
- Enough cut flowers to mark the perimeter of the circle

- A tape or CD of music for meditation

Group Ritual

All participants should place one of the flowers they brought in the basket on the altar and hold the other.

Casting the Circle

The Priestess places the flower she holds on the floor behind her as she says:
> My heart is open.

The person to her left does the same, repeating the phrase. Each person, in turn, around the circle follows suit.

Priestess   With the beauty of these gifts from Mother Earth and the magic of the sídhe, our circle is cast. We have created sacred space between the realms.

Calling the Quarters

Each participant goes to the point of the circle in their respective direction before speaking. After-wards, they light a candle on the altar. The Priest and Priestess face the altar as they speak.

North	The snowdrop, a white and green flower of hope, is first to show us that the earth is awakening. We beckon to the spirits of north, of earth to join us and sweeten our circle this night.
All	Sweeten our circle this night.
East	The carnation, sweet william, your delicate fragrance borne on gentle May breezes sweetens our lives. We beckon to the spirits of east, of air to join us and sweeten our circle this night.
All	Sweeten our circle this night.
South	The marigold is as bright and cheerful as the daystar it follows daily across the sky. We beckon to the spirits of south, of fire to join us and sweeten our circle this night.
All	Sweeten our circle this night.
West	The iris, watery blue with three inner and three outer petals is the messenger of the Goddess. We beckon to the spirits of west, of water to join us and sweeten our circle this night.
All	Sweeten our circle this night.
Priest	The rose is the king of flowers. It is said that as a spirit passes from this realm it can only be accompanied by the rose. We beckon to the Lord to join us and sweeten our circle this night.
All	Sweeten our circle this night.
Priestess	The lily, symbol of hope and grace, represents the triple ideal. We beckon to the Lady to join us and sweeten our circle this night.
All	Sweeten our circle this night.

Background

Share both Parts I and II of the background information here. The Priestess takes the bowl from the altar and gives each participant a pinch of flower seeds as the Priest reads.

Priestess   When you return to your place in the circle, observe the flower you have chosen. Flowers are delicate and beautiful and serve to remind us that we need to be gentle with ourselves and to be able to find the beauty within.

Flowers are a symbol; they show us that we need to allow ourselves to blossom and open. We must open in order to bring our special gifts to the world and to receive from others—from people we know as well as those from other realms.

Priest   Let your heart open as we move deosil around our circle and chant:

> My heart is open,
> With these words spoken,
> In a vision of love this spell
> Will not be broken.

After the energy has reached a peak and been released, the Priest and Priestess slow, then bring the activity to stillness.

Priestess   It is time to move back to our everyday world. These flowers, newly plucked from the earth, will help bring your energy to ground as you seek balance. Close your eyes and let your energy unwind. Let the energy of the flower and Mother Earth bring you to center. Allow yourself to remain open so you can bring your gifts to the everyday world.

As she speaks, the Priestess goes around the outside of the circle placing a small bundle tied with ribbon beside each flower that forms the circle. She then says:

When you are ready, open your eyes.

Closing

Each participant extinguishes a candle after speaking.

Priestess   Lady of All, we thank you for the gift of beauty that you bestow upon the world. Each time we gaze upon a flower we will remember that your fair hand created it. We ask that you bless us as you depart to your realm of beauty. Farewell, dear Lady.

All   Farewell and blessed be.

Priest   Lord of All, we thank you for the gift of mystery that you bestow upon the world. Each time a flower's fragrance envelops us we will remember that you helped create it. We ask that you bless us as you depart to your sweetly scented realm. Farewell, dear Lord.

All   Farewell and blessed be.

West   Spirits of west, messengers of the Divine, we ask that you bless us as you depart to your watery realm. Farewell, dear spirits.

All   Farewell and blessed be.

South   Spirits of south, servant of the daystar, we ask that you bless us as you depart to your fiery realm. Farewell, dear spirits.

All   Farewell and blessed be.

East   Spirits of east, sweetly scented breezes, we ask that you bless us as you depart to your airy realm. Farewell, dear spirits.

All   Farewell and blessed be.

North   Spirits of north, life-sustaining foundation, we ask that you bless us as you depart to your earthly realm. Farewell, dear spirits.

All   Farewell and blessed be.

Priestess As you retrieve the flower you placed on the floor, also receive this small gift as a reminder to be open and gentle as a flower. The sachet contains the seeds of morning glories and moon flowers so that your days and nights may be sweetly scented. Like morning glories, may you greet each day with freshness. Like moon flowers, may you find the power of Luna always within you.

Everyone joins hands around the circle, and says:
Merry meet, merry part, and merry meet again.

Solo Ritual

Casting the Circle

With the basket of cut flowers, walk the perimeter (deosil) of your circle, placing flowers at intervals along the floor. When you arrive back where you started, say:

With these gifts from the Mother,
And the magic of the sídhe,
I pass from one realm to another,
Sacred this space, I decree.

Calling the Quarters

Face each direction as you speak, and then light a candle. For the Goddess and God, face the altar.

Speak   The snowdrop, a white and green flower of hope, is first to show that the earth is awakening. I beckon to the spirits of north, of earth to join me and sweeten my circle this night.

The carnation, sweet william, your delicate fragrance borne on gentle May breezes sweetens my life. I beckon to the spirits of east, of air to join me and sweeten my circle this night.

The marigold is as bright and cheerful as the daystar it follows daily across the sky. I beckon to the spirits of south, of fire to join me and sweeten my circle this night.

The iris, watery blue with three inner and three outer petals is the messenger of the Goddess. I beckon to the spirits of west, of water to join me and sweeten my circle this night.

The rose is the king of flowers. It is said that as a spirit passes from this realm it can only be accompanied by the rose. I beckon to the Lord to join me and sweeten my circle this night.

The lily, symbol of hope and grace, represents the triple ideal. I beckon to the Lady to join me and sweeten my circle this night.

Background

Read Part I of the background. You may want to spend a little time meditating with music, and then read Part II.

When you have fixed in your mind the image of your spirit opening, go to the altar and place the seeds in the cauldron. The cauldron is an ancient symbol of the womb and of transformation. After you have placed the seeds in the cauldron, take a flower from the basket. Think of it as a precious gift.

Observe the flower. Let it be a symbol to show you the need to allow yourself to blossom and open. Be open to bring your special gifts to the world and to receive from others—from the people you know as well as those from other realms.

Let your heart open as you move deosil around the circle and chant:

My heart is open,
With these words spoken,
In a vision of love this spell
Will not be broken.

When it feels appropriate, bring the chanting and movement to stillness. Use your usual method for grounding energy.

Closing

Extinguish each candle, respectively, after speaking.

Speak   Lady of All, I thank you for the gift of beauty that you bestow upon the world. Each time I gaze upon a flower I will remember that your fair hand created it. I ask that you bless me as you depart to your realm of beauty. Farewell, dear Lady.

Lord of All, I thank you for the gift of mystery that you bestow upon the world. Each time a flower's fragrance envelops me, I will remember that you helped create it. I ask that you bless me as you depart to your sweetly scented realm. Farewell, dear Lord.

Spirits of west, messengers of the Divine, I ask that you bless me as you depart to your watery realm. Farewell, dear spirits.

Spirits of south, servant of the daystar, I ask that you bless me as you depart to your fiery realm. Farewell, dear spirits.

Spirits of east, sweetly scented breezes, I ask that you bless me as you depart to your airy realm. Farewell, dear spirits.

Spirits of north, life-sustaining foundation, I ask that you bless me as you depart to your earthly realm. Farewell, dear spirits.

Take the sachet and hold it in your hands as you face the altar.

Speak   Thank you for this gift which will be a reminder for me to be open and gentle as a flower. May these seeds of morning glories and moon flowers bring sweetness to my days and nights. Like morning glories, may I greet each day with freshness. Like moon flowers, may I find the power of Luna always within me. In faith and unity, blessed be.

MOON OF LIFE

June

Before the heat of high summer arrives, there is a brief period of time to enjoy the softness of this season. Tune into the rhythms of the natural world and take pleasure in your connection with it. Go outside and let the energy of the moonlight help you feel fully alive and aware. Enjoy the magic of gentle moonlight on soft summer nights.

Other Names for This Moon

- Mead Moon
- Dyad Moon
- Honey Moon
- Strawberry Moon

In the Celtic Tree Calendar

June 1–9: Hawthorne—associated with balancing energy; it is a symbol of the coming summer, and of hope and pleasure.

June 10–30: Oak—associated with cleansing, strength, self-confidence, and optimism.

Background for This Ritual

Solo practitioners will want to read this just before beginning the ritual. A place has been indicated in the group ritual where this is most appropriate for the Priestess or Priest to share with everyone:

> In June we enjoy the longest days of the year, especially before the summer solstice. Even though the sun begins to withdraw after the solstice, the shortening of days is imperceptible and we enjoy long hours of light. This is a time to be active, to feel sensuous, and to be aware of our bodies and the lifeforce energy that flows through us. As the Wheel of the Year moves into summer, we raise the heat of this new season with both a drumming circle and a circle dance.
>
> The circle is one of the oldest and most elemental symbols. It is also a symbol of perfection and wholeness. It represents unity and endlessness. It echoes the recurring cycles of life and death and rebirth, of the sun and moon and seasons. The circle reminds us that all events, all life, and everything in the universe is connected in a perpetual flow of energy. With a circle dance, power and strength is evoked.
>
> The drum is one of the oldest musical instruments known. In ancient cultures drumming was a sacred function. The rhythm of drumming and dancing connects us with nature and the heartbeat of life.

Themes

- Enjoy long days and summer warmth.
- Use dancing and drumming to be fully in your physical self.
- Celebrate the energy of life.

Drum Sounds

Use these distinct sounds just before evoking each direction. In the group ritual, the participants can do their own drumming before speaking or the Priest or Priestess may do it for them.

- **North:** Slap a hand against the center of the drumhead (avoiding a resonating sound) in a slow rhythm.

- **East:** Brush a finger over the drumhead in a circular motion.

- **South:** With a drumstick, make a staccato rhythm at the edge of the drumhead.

- **West:** With a drumstick, create a deep resonating rhythm in the center of the drumhead.

Preparation

Items needed for this ritual include the following:

- Drums or other percussion instruments, furnished by the participants

- Chalice and small paper cups for those who may not want to drink from the chalice

- Mead or a honeyed tea such as chamomile

Group Ritual

Casting the Circle

Priestess   This is the soft time of summer, a time to feel the vital rhythm of life. We cast our circle by naming ourselves and playing a drum.

After saying her name, the Priestess taps out a brief rhythm and then hands the drum to the person on her left. Each participant follows suit with his or her own rhythm. When the drum arrives back to the Priestess, she says:

With our names and rhythms we have made this space sacred. This circle represents our entering into a new season of warmth and light that encourages growth. This is a circle built with the pulse of life.

Calling the Quarters

Each participant stands in his or her respective direction with a drum. The Priest and Priestess stand at the altar.

North   [*Drumming*] We call ye spirits of north, of earth to join our celebration of life.

All   Be with us this night.

East   [*Drumming*] We call ye spirits of east, of air to join our celebration of life.

All	Be with us this night.
South	[*Drumming*] We call ye spirits of south, of fire to join our celebration of life.
All	Be with us this night.
West	[*Drumming*] We call ye spirits of west, of water to join our celebration of life.
All	Be with us this night.

Together the Priest and Priestess create a rhythm and counter-rhythm on their drums, and then say:

Priest	We call the Lord.
Priestess	We call the Lady.
In unison	Join our celebration of life.
All	Be with us this night.

Background

As the Priestess and Priest share the background information, a helper lightly brushes his or her finger over a drum in a circular motion to create a gentle sound.

Priestess	You may choose to dance, drum, or do both. Follow what is appropriate for you. Once the drumming begins, we will move deosil around the altar.

The Priest and Priestess begin a rhythm; others may initiate a counter-rhythm. The Priest, Priestess, or a helper initiates the dancing. Those leading these activities should be able to cue each other when it seems appropriate to slow and then end the drumming and dancing.

When the activity is brought to stillness, the Priestess says:

May our celebration of summer send a ripple of joy out to the world.

Priest	You may want to sit on the floor to help bring your energy level down. Close your eyes for a moment. Take a deep breath and feel your connection to Mother Earth. Feel your excess energy flow to her and know that

when you need extra energy, it will be there for you. When you are ready, open your eyes.

The Priest takes a chalice of mead or honeyed tea from the altar and says:
> In this time of the Mead Moon, the Honey Moon, the Moon of Life, we share this drink to celebrate summer.

He raises the chalice to a participant's lips and says:
> Enjoy the bright days of summer that stretch before us.

Each person in turn raises the chalice to the person on his or her left and repeats the phrase. When it goes around the circle and comes back to the Priest, he offers it to the Priestess who then offers it to him.

Closing

Each participant faces his or her respective direction. The Priest and Priestess face the altar.

Priestess   Lord and Lady, we thank you for the gift of life and the enjoyment it brings.

Priest   Thank you for your presence in our circle. Stay if you will, go if you must. We bid you farewell.

All   We bid you farewell. Blessed be.

West   Spirits of west, we thank you for the resonant rhythms of the ocean. Thank you for your presence in our circle. Stay if you will, go if you must. We bid you farewell.

All   We bid you farewell. Blessed be.

South   Spirits of south, we thank you for the crackling staccato of fire. Thank you for your presence in our circle. Stay if you will, go if you must. We bid you farewell.

All   We bid you farewell. Blessed be.

East   Spirits of east, we thank you for the gentle sighing of air. Thank you for your presence in our circle. Stay if you will, go if you must. We bid you farewell.

All   We bid you farewell. Blessed be.

North   Spirits of north, we thank you for the deep rhythm of earth. Thank you for your presence in our circle. Stay if you will, go if you must. We bid you farewell.

All   We bid you farewell. Blessed be.

Everyone joins hands.

Priestess   As we return to the rhythm of our everyday lives, may we carry within us the call of nature's rhythms that connect us with the web of all life.

All   Merry meet, merry part, and merry meet again.

Solo Ritual

Casting the Circle

As you walk around the perimeter of your circle, lightly brush a finger over your drum in a circular motion to create a gentle sound.

Speak

As I feel the warm sun on my face,

The rhythm of life beats a fast pace,

It is time to dance and feel free,

Sacred this space, I now decree.

Calling the Quarters

Move to each direction, respectively. For the Lord and Lady, stand at the altar.

Speak   [*Drumming*] I call ye spirits of north, of earth to join my celebration of life.

             [*Drumming*] I call ye spirits of east, of air to join my celebration of life.

             [*Drumming*] I call ye spirits of south, of fire to join my celebration of life.

             [*Drumming*] I call ye spirits of west, of water to join my celebration of life.

Alternate a rhythm and counter-rhythm, and then say:

> I call the Lord. I call the Lady. Join my celebration of life.

Begin drumming and moving deosil around your altar. Become fully engaged in the rhythm and allow your consciousness to shift inward. You may find that you begin to journey. Go with the energy flow as it may reveal information you need at this point in your life.

When it feels appropriate, bring your journey to a conclusion and your activity to stillness. Say:

> May my celebration of summer send a ripple of joy out to the world.

Use your usual method of grounding energy.

Take the chalice of mead or honeyed tea from the altar and say:

> In this time of the Mead Moon, the Honey Moon, the Moon of Life, I drink this to celebrate summer. I will enjoy the bright days of summer that stretch before me.

Closing

Begin at the altar, and then face each direction respectively. After speaking each part, briefly beat your drum.

Speak   Lord and Lady, I thank you for the gift of life and the enjoyment it brings. Thank you for your presence in my circle. Stay if you will, go if you must. I bid you farewell.

Spirits of west, I thank you for the resonant rhythms of the ocean. Thank you for your presence in my circle. Stay if you will, go if you must. I bid you farewell.

Spirits of south, I thank you for the crackling staccato of fire. Thank you for your presence in my circle. Stay if you will, go if you must. I bid you farewell.

Spirits of east, I thank you for the gentle sighing of air. Thank you for your presence in my circle. Stay if you will, go if you must. I bid you farewell.

Spirits of north, I thank you for the deep rhythm of earth. Thank you for your presence in my circle. Stay if you will, go if you must. I bid you farewell.

My circle is open but unbroken,
No longer sacred, this space I decree.
Words of the Goddess have been spoken,
In faith and unity, blessed be.

MOON OF FIRE

July

Shimmering waves of heat rise skyward during the day, and night does not always bring cooling relief. The Moon of Fire reminds us that her brother, Sun, is at his peak. Bask in the heat of this season and think of the sacred flame that burns within us all.

Other Names for this Moon

- Blessing Moon

- Wort (Herb) Moon

- Thunder Moon

In the Celtic Tree Calendar

July 1–7: Oak—associated with the power of vision, self-confidence.

July 8–31: Holly—associated with hearth and home; along with oak, holly was one of the trees favored by the Druids for their sacred groves.

Background for This Ritual

Solo practitioners: read Part I just before beginning and Part II where indicated in the ritual. A place has been indicated in the group ritual where Parts I and II are most appropriate for the Priestess or Priest to share with everyone:

Part I: Civilization cannot exist without fire. Civilization did not begin until wild fire was tamed into the hearth fire. But while we humans may be able to contain fire, we cannot completely control it. Therein lies its mystery— fire has power that is beyond us. It has a power that we watch with fear and awe. It is easy to be mesmerized by it.

Tamed fire is the hearth. It is welcoming and protective. It provides warmth. But tamed fire also tamed humans. Nomadic peoples became settled communities when they could grow grain and bake bread. And fire is the alchemist that transforms minerals into tools.

Fire embodies the essence of natural cycles: destruction brings about creation. Symbolically, the phoenix rises from the ashes, transformed by the flames. And so fire is a powerful symbol of rebirth, immortality, and purification.

Fire is linked with the sacred. It represents the Divine spark of life. We speak of our inner fire. Fire is the element linked with the heart chakra. And fire is the symbol of love, of burning passion. Fire is illumination and the spark of inspiration.

Fire produces light, but in doing so it creates shadow and therein is the symbol of its cycle: destruction, healing, transformation, inspiration. Fire can symbolically clear our spiritual paths of obstacles. It can reduce what is unneeded to ash, giving us room to heal. But it cannot do this without our letting go of whatever holds us back. Letting go, symbolically walking into the sacred flame, allows us to transform, to move on. With this freedom comes inspiration and growth. Like a forest that springs back to life after being destroyed, our souls revive when we let go, allowing transformation to happen.

Part II: We think of holly as relating to Yule, but holly is the Celtic tree month that comprises most of July because it flowers at this time of year. It is in the winter around Yule time that it bears fruit, and so holly represents commitment to something that will come to fruition later. Holly, like fire, represents faith.

We will use the slips of holly-shaped paper to make a vow, a commitment to ourselves. Write on the paper what it is you need to release from your life, what you need to make a commitment to in order to move forward. It may have to do with your family, your career, your faith. Make a note about some form of transformation needed in your life. You only need to jot down a word or two. The important thing is to fix the intention in your mind and let the paper represent what is to be released.

Themes

- Acknowledge fire and its importance to civilization.

- Honor sacred flame and its power of transformation.

- Use the image of fire to symbolize release and renewal.

Preparation

Items needed for this ritual include the following:

- One candle in a holder that can be safely placed on the floor, provided by each participant

- One piece of paper cut into the shape of a holly leaf approximately 2 x 3 inches for each participant

- One pencil for each participant

- Six red candles for the altar

- Cauldron

- Drums and/or other percussion instruments to accompany chanting (optional)

FOR SOLO RITUAL

- Candles to place around the perimeter of your circle

Group Ritual

Priestess   As sunlight slants across fields of golden grain, we gather in the heat of July, in the sultry heat of high summer to celebrate sacred fire. Fire has great powers of destruction, but it also has powers of healing and transformation.

Casting the Circle

Each participant holds his or her candle. The Priestess goes to the altar and lights her own candle. Facing the altar, she raises it and says:

> We call to the sacred fire, hearth fire, flame within our souls.

With the candle, she returns to her place in the circle and touches the flame of it to the candle of the person on her left, saying:

> With fire we cast our circle.

Each participant, in turn, repeats the phrase as he or she lights candles around the circle. When everyone's candle is lit, the Priestess says:

> With sacred fire, our circle is cast.

All   So mote it be.

Calling the Quarters

Each person faces his or her respective direction while speaking, and then lights one of the red candles on the altar. The Priest and Priestess face the altar when they speak.

North   We summon ye spirits of north, of earth. Be the foundation beneath the ashes of the sacred flame of Brigid. We welcome you to our bright circle.

All   We welcome you to our bright circle.

East   We summon ye spirits of east, of air. Be the gentle whisper that ignites the spark of the sacred flame of Brigid. We welcome you to our bright circle.

All   We welcome you to our bright circle.

South   We summon ye spirits of south, of fire. We call on your powers to build the sacred flame of Brigid. We welcome you to our bright circle.

All   We welcome you to our bright circle.

West   We summon ye spirits of west, of water. Be the holy well that balances the sacred flame of Brigid. We welcome you to our bright circle.

All   We welcome you to our bright circle.

Priest	This is the flame of destruction, the flame of purification. Lord of All, Lugh, we ask that you guide us through the fire. We welcome you to our bright circle.
All	We welcome you to our bright circle.
Priestess	This is the flame of healing, the flame of transformation. Lady of All, Brigid, we ask that you guide us through the fire. We welcome you to our bright circle.
All	We welcome you to our bright circle.

Background

Share Part I of the background information here.

Priest	Give thought to what you may need to release from your life in order to move forward. Is there some sort of obstacle holding you back?

The Priestess passes around the pencils and paper shaped like holly leaves. Holding up one of the pieces of paper, she shares Part II of the background information here.

Priest	Once we begin the chant, and when you are ready, come to the altar and say what you want to release and transform in your life. Carefully, pass the paper through the candle flame, then drop it into the cauldron and feel freedom as the paper is reduced to ash.
Chant	Fire in the night. Burning, burning, burning. Guide us with your light. Burning, burning, burning. Transforming with your flame. Burning, burning, burning. That which I have named. Burning, burning, burning.[1]

Participants may choose to drum and/or move around the circle while chanting. When everyone has burned their papers, the Priest and Priestess slow the chanting, drumming, and dancing, and then bring it to a halt.

| Priest | Take a deep breath and close your eyes. Feel the heat of your energy begin to slow. Let it flow down through your body. Let the ashes of what you have released return to Mother Earth. Let her balancing energy return you to center. When you are ready, open your eyes. |

Closing

Each participant faces his or her respective direction and extinguishes the candle he or she lit.

Priestess	Lady of All, dear Brigid, thank you for this transformation and for your presence in our bright circle this night. We ask for your blessing as you depart, and bid you farewell.
All	We bid you farewell. Blessed be.
Priest	Lord of All, dear Lugh, thank you for your inspiration and for your presence in our bright circle this night. We ask for your blessing as you depart, and bid you farewell.
All	We bid you farewell. Blessed be.
West	Spirits of west, of water, thank you for your balance and for your presence in our bright circle this night. We ask for your blessing as you depart, and bid you farewell.
All	We bid you farewell. Blessed be.
South	Spirits of south, of fire, thank you for your power and for your presence in our bright circle this night. We ask for your blessing as you depart, and bid you farewell.
All	We bid you farewell. Blessed be.
East	Spirits of east, of air, thank you for your gentle whisper and for your presence in our bright circle this night. We ask for your blessing as you depart, and bid you farewell.
All	We bid you farewell. Blessed be.

North	Spirits of north, of earth, thank you for your foundation and for your presence in our bright circle this night. We ask for your blessing as you depart, and bid you farewell.

All	We bid you farewell. Blessed be.

Everyone picks up his or her candle from the floor.

Priestess	By the flame of destruction and transformation we are strengthened and set free. May the sacred flame of inspiration and wisdom remain in our hearts.

Participants extinguish their candles.

All	Merry meet, merry part, and merry meet again.

Solo Ritual

Casting the Circle

Light a candle (not one of the six red altar candles), and then walk around the perimeter of your circle lighting the candles you placed on the floor.

Speak	Sacred circle, sacred fire, I beckon you to inspire. With your power bring to me Light and wisdom, so mote it be.

Calling the Quarters

Face each direction as you speak, and then light one of the red candles on the altar. For the Goddess and God, face the altar.

Speak	I summon ye spirits of north, of earth. Be the foundation beneath the ashes of the sacred flame of Brigid. I welcome you to my bright circle. I summon ye spirits of east, of air. Be the gentle whisper that ignites the spark of the sacred flame of Brigid. I welcome you to my bright circle. I summon ye spirits of south, of fire. I call on your powers to build the sacred flame of Brigid. I welcome you to my bright circle.

I summon ye spirits of west, of water. Be the holy well that balances the sacred flame of Brigid. I welcome you to my bright circle.

This is the flame of destruction, the flame of purification. Lord of All, Lugh, I ask that you guide me through the fire. I welcome you to my bright circle.

This is the flame of healing, the flame of transformation. Lady of All, Brigid, I ask that you guide me through the fire. I welcome you to my bright circle.

Background

Read Part II of the background information here.

Give thought to what you may need to release from your life in order to move forward. Is there an obstacle holding you back? Take the holly-shaped paper. Write on it what you need to release from your life, what you need to make a commitment to in order to move forward.

Begin the chant as you think about your intention. When you are ready, pause and then state what you want to release and transform in your life. Carefully, pass the paper through the candle flame and say:

I acknowledge _____ and let it go.

Drop the paper into the cauldron and feel freedom as the paper is reduced to ash. Resume chanting. Also drum and/or move around your circle, if you choose.

Chant

Fire in the night.
Burning, burning, burning.
Guide me with your light.
Burning, burning, burning.
Transforming with your flame.
Burning, burning, burning.
That which I have named.
Burning, burning, burning.

When it feels appropriate, bring your chanting (drumming and movement) to stillness. Use your usual methods for grounding energy.

Closing

Stand facing each direction as you speak, and then extinguish its related altar candle. For the Goddess and God, face the altar.

Speak   Lady of All, dear Brigid, thank you for this transformation and for your presence in my bright circle this night. I ask for your blessing as you depart, and bid you farewell.

Lord of All, dear Lugh, thank you for your inspiration and for your presence in my bright circle this night. I ask for your blessing as you depart, and bid you farewell.

Spirits of west, of water, thank you for your balance and for your presence in my bright circle this night. I ask for your blessing as you depart, and bid you farewell.

Spirits of south, of fire, thank you for your power and for your presence in my bright circle this night. I ask for your blessing as you depart, and bid you farewell.

Spirits of east, of air, thank you for your gentle whisper and for your presence in my bright circle this night. I ask for your blessing as you depart, and bid you farewell.

Spirits of north, of earth, thank you for your foundation and for your presence in my bright circle this night. I ask for your blessing as you depart, and bid you farewell.

As you go around the perimeter of your circle extinguishing candles, say:

> By the flame of destruction and transformation,
> I am strengthened and set free.
> May the flame of inspiration and wisdom,
> Burn within and stay with me.

---

1. This chant can be done as a call-and-answer with one group singing just the "Burning, burning, burning" lines.

MOON OF DELIGHT

August

Lazy days are offset by dazzling thunderstorms that tear the night sky asunder. Summer is winding down and yet autumn seems a distant horizon. This is the time to enjoy the warmth, the freedom of lightweight clothing, and the night chorus of crickets as you recall pleasant summer memories.

Other Names for This Moon

- Herb Moon
- Barley Moon
- Corn Moon

In the Celtic Tree Calendar

August 1–4: Holly—associated with unity, energy, guidance for the future, and the waning year.

August 5–31: Hazel—associated with creativity, wisdom, authority, and justice.

Background for This Ritual

Places have been indicated in both the group and solo rituals where Parts I and II are most appropriate to read:

Part I: One of our themes tonight is water. For our ancestors, water was vital to ensure a bountiful harvest, which would secure their future, their survival. This is true for us too, but if we have a drought in our area, food can be brought in (and usually is anyway) from other areas.

Summer showers give us respite from hot afternoons, and water more than anything else deeply quenches our thirst. Tonight the chalice is used to enjoy a drink of cool, clear springwater.

Part II: For us in the twenty-first century, water and summer are also linked but we mainly think about pleasure. We visit the beach or go swimming in pools and ponds. For us, summer is a time to relax and get outdoors, and so we all have memories and joys associated with summer.

Many of these memories probably come from childhood when summertime seemed to stretch on forever and playing out of doors after dark was magic.

Themes

- Recognize the importance of water to our ancestors.

- Recall summer pleasures and memories.

Preparation

Items needed for this ritual include the following:

- Four candles for the altar for the directions/elements (choose colors appropriate for your tradition or see Table 2 in appendix A)

- A brown or gold candle for the God and a black candle for the Goddess

- Chalice and small paper cups for those who may not want to drink from the chalice

- Springwater

- Enough twelve-inch pieces of yarn in the colors of the four directions/elements for each participant to take several colors

OPTIONAL
- Potted, fresh-cut, or dried herbs to decorate the altar

Also, solo practitioners may want to mark the perimeter of their circles with objects that symbolize summer such as seashells, a pair of sandals, sunglasses, etc. Decorative jars partially filled with springwater would also be appropriate for this ritual.

Group Ritual

Casting the Circle

Priestess   We cast our circle in this sultry month of August by joining hands. Hand to hand the circle is cast.

Each participant repeats the phrase as he or she takes the hand of the person on his or her left. When the circle is connected, the Priestess says:

With this circle, symbol of strength and unity, we have created sacred space where the realms touch.

Calling the Quarters

Each participant walks to the edge of the circle in his or her respective direction, and then lights a candle on the altar after speaking. The Priest and Priestess stand in front of the altar to evoke deity.

North   Hark, ye spirits of north, of earth. We rejoice in your verdant fields, orchards, and thick forests. We light this green candle to symbolize the green earth. Spirits of earth be with us this night

All   Spirits of earth be with us this night.

East   Hark, ye spirits of east, of air. We revel in the stillness of warm afternoons when birds soar high to touch the clouds. We light this yellow candle to symbolize the bright, sun-filled sky. Spirits of air, be with us this night.

All   Spirits of air, be with us this night.

South   Hark, ye spirits of south, of fire. We delight in long sultry days that unfold slowly to a symphony of cicadas that herald the sun's path through the sky. We light this red candle to symbolize the glowing heat of summer. Spirits of fire, be with us this night.

All	Spirits of fire, be with us this night.
West	Hark, ye spirits of west, of water. We savor the sudden showers that quench the thirsty soil and refresh lakes and streams. We light this blue candle to symbolize the cooling gentle rain. Spirits of water, be with us this night.
All	Spirits of water, be with us this night.
Priest	Lugh, Green Man, this is the height of your vitality. The full strength of your lifeforce is evident in all we see. We light this brown candle to symbolize the ripening grain. Lord of All, be with us this night.
All	Lord of All, be with us this night.
Priestess	Brigid, Demeter, your nurturing presence gives us comfort to enjoy the beauty that surrounds us. We light this black candle to symbolize the rich fertile soil of Mother Gaia. Lady of All, be with us this night.
All	Lady of All, be with us this night.

Background

Share Part I of the background information here.

> *The Priestess takes the chalice from the altar and gives the person to her left a drink, saying:*
> Partake of this life-giving water. Let it nourish your body and soul.

> *Each participant repeats this phrase as he or she offers water to the next person. When the chalice comes back to the Priestess, she goes to the altar, and says:*
> Lord and Lady, we thank you for the gift of this water.

Background

Share Part II of the background information here.

Priest	Think of one of your fond summer memories or joys that you would like to share with the group. As you think about it, we are going to weave our part of a web of summer joys. Take several strands of yarn in whatever colors are appropriate to an element or two related to your summer joy.

Braid or weave or tie the pieces of yarn together in any way you want as you think of summer.

As we do this we will chant:

Weaving memories, to and fro,
Braiding lifetimes as we go.

When participants have finished their braids and knots, the Priestess brings the chanting to an end, and says:

One by one we will go around the circle and tell about our summer memories. After speaking, the first person will pass his or her yarn to the person on the left who will tie his or hers onto it while sharing his or her experience. Each person will pass on the yarn and when we end we will have a web of summer memories.

The Priest or Priestess may want to begin the sharing. After everyone has spoken and added their braid to the web, the Priestess says:

Now we will pass the web around the circle and chant again. Hold the yarn for a moment or two and feel the power of the joys we have woven into this web of memories.

After the yarn web has been passed around the circle, the Priest or Priestess slows, then ends the chanting and places the yarn on the altar, saying:

Lord and Lady, we offer you our joys and pleasant memories of summer.

All   Blessed be.

Priest   It is time to bring our ritual to an end. Close your eyes and let the energy unwind. As you feel it spiral down, let it connect with Mother Earth. Feel the slow energy of summer. Let our circle of sharing become part of a new summer memory for you. When you are ready, open your eyes.

Closing

After speaking, each participant, in turn, puts out the candle he or she lit at the beginning of the ritual.

Priestess	Great Lady, thank you for your nurturing love and the joys of summer. We ask for your blessing as you depart. Stay if you will, go if you must. Farewell. Blessed be.
All	Farewell and blessed be.
Priest	Great Lord, thank you for the vitality of these active summer months. We ask for your blessing as you depart. Stay if you will, go if you must. Farewell. Blessed be.
All	Farewell and blessed be.
West	Spirits of west, of water, thank you for your cooling summer rains. We ask for your blessing as you depart. Stay if you will, go if you must. Farewell. Blessed be.
All	Farewell and blessed be.
South	Spirits of south, of fire, thank you for the heat that ripens the fields. We ask for your blessing as you depart. Stay if you will, go if you must. Farewell. Blessed be.
All	Farewell and blessed be.
East	Spirits of east, of air, thank you for the clear bright summer skies. We ask for your blessing as you depart. Stay if you will, go if you must. Farewell. Blessed be.
All	Farewell and blessed be.
North	Spirits of north, of earth, thank you for the beauty of the land. We ask for your blessing as you depart. Stay if you will, go if you must. Farewell. Blessed be.
All	Farewell and blessed be.

Everyone joins hands.

Priestess   Recall what you have shared this night and take time for your own inner celebration of summer. Know that you carry it with you. Our circle of summer memories is now open but unbroken.

All   Merry meet, merry part, and merry meet again.

Solo Ritual

Casting the Circle

Walk around the perimeter of your circle as you say:

> Joyous summer, day heart-free,
> Ripening fields and shining sea.
> Sacred space, I now decree,
> Mother Goddess, I welcome thee.

Calling the Quarters

Walk to the edge of the circle in the respective direction as you call each. After speaking, light a candle on the altar. Stand in front of the altar to evoke the Goddess and God.

Speak   Hark, ye spirits of north, of earth. I rejoice in your verdant fields, orchards, and thick forests. Tonight I light this green candle to symbolize the green earth. Spirits of earth be with me.

Hark, ye spirits of east, of air. I revel in the stillness of warm afternoons when birds soar high to touch the clouds. Tonight I light this yellow candle to symbolize the bright, sun-filled sky. Spirits of air, be with me.

Hark, ye spirits of south, of fire. I delight in long sultry days that unfold slowly to a symphony of cicadas that herald the sun's path through the sky. Tonight I light this red candle to symbolize the glowing heat of summer. Spirits of fire, be with me.

Hark, ye spirits of west, of water. I savor the sudden showers that quench the thirsty soil and refresh lakes and streams. Tonight I light this blue candle to symbolize the cooling gentle rain. Spirits of water, be with me.

Lugh, Green Man, this is the height of your vitality. The full strength of your lifeforce is evident in all I see. Tonight I light this brown candle to symbolize the ripening grain. Lord of All, be with me.

Brigid, Demeter, your nurturing presence gives me comfort to enjoy the beauty that surrounds me. Tonight I light this black candle to symbolize the rich fertile soil of Mother Gaia. Lady of All, be with me.

Background

Read Part I.

Contemplate the importance of water. Fill your chalice with cool, clear springwater. Before drinking, say:

I partake of this life-giving water. Let it nourish my body and soul. Lord and Lady, thank you for the gift of this water.

Background

Read Part II here.

Think of what you enjoy most about summer as well as memories of special things and events. As you think of each summer pleasure or memory, take several strands of yarn in whatever colors are appropriate to an element or two related to it. Braid, weave, or tie the pieces of yarn together as you think of summer. Create a web of summer memories. As you do so, chant:

Weaving memories, to and fro,
Braiding lifetimes as I go.

When you are finished braiding and tying pieces together, hold the yarn and feel the power of the joy you have woven into this web of memories. When you are ready, lay it on your altar, and say:

Lord and Lady, I offer you my joys and pleasant summer memories. Blessed be.

Use your usual method for grounding energy.

Closing

Walk to the edge of the circle in the respective direction as you dismiss each. After speaking, extinguish a candle on the altar. Stand in front of the altar when addressing the Goddess and God.

Speak   Great Lady, thank you for your nurturing love and the joys of summer. I ask for your blessing as you depart. Stay if you will, go if you must. Farewell. Blessed be.

Great Lord, thank you for the vitality of these active summer months. I ask for your blessing as you depart. Stay if you will, go if you must. Farewell. Blessed be.

Spirits of west, of water, thank you for your cooling summer rains. I ask for your blessing as you depart. Stay if you will, go if you must. Farewell. Blessed be.

Spirits of south, of fire, thank you for the heat that ripens the fields. I ask for your blessing as you depart. Stay if you will, go if you must. Farewell. Blessed be.

Spirits of east, of air, thank you for the clear, bright summer skies. I ask for your blessing as you depart. Stay if you will, go if you must. Farewell. Blessed be.

Spirits of north, of earth, thank you for the beauty of the land. I ask for your blessing as you depart. Stay if you will, go if you must. Farewell. Blessed be.

Take the yarn web and carry it as you walk around your circle saying:

> Summer joys and memories glow,
> But this season soon must go.
> Let these warm thoughts stay with me,
> As time goes on, so mote it be.

MOON OF THE HARVEST

September

Most of September lies within the Celtic month of vine. It is at this time of year when fruits and vegetables that grow on vines are harvested. The vine symbolizes the twists and turns our paths may follow. It also symbolizes the (pro)active energy we need in order to make or ride out the changes in our lives.

Other Names for This Moon

- Grain Moon
- Fruit Moon
- Green Corn Moon

In the Celtic Tree Calendar

September 1: Hazel—associated with creativity, the ability to find truth.

September 2–29: Vine—associated with unstoppable energy, learning, making changes in life.

September 30: Ivy—associated with transformation, healing; it is also a symbol of love.

Background for This Ritual

A place has been indicated in both the group and solo rituals where this is most appropriate to read:

> Summer is over, yet many afternoons are still warm. And while the nights become chilly, winter's threat is not yet real. Our ancestors would be busy with the harvest, but for better or worse, we are removed from it. Most of us do not have to engage in the heavy labor of harvest, but the trade-off is that most of us no longer live close to the land.
>
> We should consider the time and conveniences of our modern lives a gift. This time we share together and our time in ritual are also gifts. Each of us has something to offer, and so tonight we will offer our gifts.
>
> Nature also has many gifts to offer and tonight we combine these with ours. The acorn is a tiny thing that holds great promise for the future. From something so small comes something great. It offers strength and endurance. Tonight these acorns will be symbolic of the gifts we offer the world.
>
> Cup the acorns between your palms. Let your thoughts and energy flow into them as you think of what you wish for others. You may wish someone the gift of good health, you may offer the gift of your friendship, or you may wish that a person receive the strength to deal with a challenge in his or her life.

Themes

- Celebrate the harvest.

- Acknowledge this time of abundance as a time for spiritually gathering in.

- Take time for sharing.

Preparation

Items needed for this ritual include the following:

- Six candles for the altar

- A bowl of acorns containing enough for each participant to be given a handful

- Vines, real or artificial, to decorate the altar (optional)

- Tape or CD to play during the core part of the ritual with which people can sing or drum (optional)

- Drums or other percussion instruments (optional)

Group Ritual

Priestess   This is the Moon of the Harvest. This is a time for gathering in and drawing abundance into our lives. But in accumulating wealth of any sort or prosperity of any amount, it is important to share. Tonight's ritual is about the gifts we receive as well as the gifts we give.

Casting the Circle

Priestess   We cast our circle by naming ourselves. I am _____.

As the Priestess says her name, she takes the hand of the person on her left. Each person in turn gives his or her name while taking the next person's hand. Participants with magic or coven names may choose to use these. When everyone has joined hands, the Priestess says:

With the power of our names, this circle is cast. We have passed through the gateway between the worlds.

Calling the Quarters

Each participant walks to the edge of the circle in his or her respective direction, then lights a candle on the altar after speaking. The Priest and Priestess stand in front of the altar to evoke deity.

North   We call to the north, to earth, and invite you to our circle with your gifts of endurance, everyday existence, and foundation. Be with us as the roots that connect us to sacred places. Spirits of earth, be with us this night.

All   Spirits of earth, be with us this night.

East   We call to the east, to air, and invite you to our circle with your gifts of awareness, communication, and inspiration. Be with us as the soft voice of nature. Spirits of air, be with us this night.

All   Spirits of air, be with us this night.

South	We call to the south, to fire, and invite you to our circle with your gifts of strength, sensation, and courage. Be with us as the catalyst for transformation. Spirits of fire, be with us this night.
All	Spirits of fire, be with us this night.
West	We call to the west, to water, and invite you to our circle with your gifts of emotion, intuition, and receptivity. Be with us as the guide for our dreams and self-discovery. Spirits of water, be with us this night.
All	Spirits of water, be with us this night.
Priest	We call to the Lord, God of All, and invite you to our circle with your gifts of everlasting vitality and the spark of life that brings the world into being. Lord of All, be with us this night.
All	Lord of All, be with us this night.
Priestess	We call to the Lady, Goddess of All, and invite you to our circle with your gifts of the powers of earth and the mystery of sister Luna. Lady of All, be with us this night.
All	Lady of All, be with us this night.

Background

Share the background information here. As the Priest speaks, the Priestess takes the bowl of acorns from the altar and begins to distribute them to the participants.

Priest	When you are ready, go to someone in this circle. Tell that person what gift you offer or wish for him or her and give the person one of your acorns. It is not necessary that you both exchange gifts or that you do so at the same time. You can go on to someone else and then return to a person. These acorns will get passed around the group and acquire the energy of many gifts.

If you are using a tape or CD, start it now. When the activity of exchanging acorns/gifts begins to wind down, the Priest and Priestess stop the music and bring any singing or drumming to an end.

Priestess	Cup the acorns that you now hold between your palms in front of your chest. Feel the energy and love of the gifts each acorn represents. Feel that energy in your heart chakra. Feel the love and caring of this community.
Priest	It is now time to move back to our everyday world. Close your eyes and let the energy that has been raised return to Mother Earth. As you feel it spiral down, touch your energy to Mother Earth and feel her balance. Let it bring you to center. When you are ready, open your eyes.

Closing

After speaking, each participant, in turn, puts out the candle he or she lit at the beginning of the ritual.

Priestess	Lady, Goddess of All, thank you for the gifts you bestow on us and for joining us in our circle this night. We ask for your blessing as you depart, and bid you farewell. Blessed be.
All	We bid you farewell. Blessed be.
Priest	Lord, God of All, thank you for the gifts you bestow on us and for joining us in our circle this night. We ask for your blessing as you depart, and bid you farewell. Blessed be.
All	We bid you farewell. Blessed be.
West	Spirits of west, of water, thank you for the gift of dreams and self-discovery. We ask for your blessing as you depart, and bid you farewell. Blessed be.
All	We bid you farewell. Blessed be.
South	Spirits of south, of fire, thank you for the gift of transformation. We ask for your blessing as you depart, and bid you farewell. Blessed be.
All	We bid you farewell. Blessed be.
East	Spirits of east, of air, thank you for the gift of nature's voice. We ask for your blessing as you depart, and bid you farewell. Blessed be.

All	We bid you farewell. Blessed be.
North	Spirits of north, of earth, thank you for the gift of connection with sacred places. We ask for your blessing as you depart, and bid you farewell. Blessed be.
All	We bid you farewell. Blessed be.

Everyone joins hands.

Priestess	We have given and received gifts tonight in the sacred circle. As we return to the everyday world, we will be more aware of the gifts that surround us and are available when we open our hearts.
All	Merry meet, merry part, and merry meet again.

Solo Ritual

Casting the Circle

As you walk the perimeter of your circle, say:

Harvest moon, gather in,
I draw abundance to me.
Family, friends, those in need,
I share it all with thee.
Sacred is this space decreed in this harvesttime.

Calling the Quarters

Walk to the edge of the circle in the respective direction as you call each. After speaking, light a candle on the altar. Stand in front of the altar to evoke the Goddess and God.

Speak	I call to the north, to earth, and invite you to my circle with your gifts of endurance, everyday existence, and foundation. Be with me as the roots that connect me to sacred places. Spirits of earth, be with me this night.
	I call to the east, to air, and invite you to my circle with your gifts of awareness, communication, and inspiration. Be with me as the soft voice of nature. Spirits of air, be with me this night.

I call to the south, to fire, and invite you to my circle with your gifts of strength, sensation, and courage. Be with me as the catalyst for transformation. Spirits of fire, be with me this night.

I call to the west, to water, and invite you to my circle with your gifts of emotion, intuition, and receptivity. Be with me as the guide for my dreams and self-discovery. Spirits of water, be with me this night.

I call to the Lord, God of All, and invite you to my circle with your gifts of everlasting vitality and the spark of life that brings the world into being. Lord of All, be with me this night.

I call to the Lady, Goddess of All, and invite you to my circle with your gifts of the powers of earth and the mystery of sister Luna. Lady of All, be with me this night.

Background

Read the background information here.

Walk around your altar three times, and then one by one place an acorn on it. As you place each one, say aloud to whom you are offering a gift and what that gift is. When you are finished, and to give power to the intention of your gifts, raise energy with the vine dance.

If you are using recorded music, begin it now, and then begin your dance. Your left leg advances your step. Your right leg will move first, behind then in front of the left to simulate the winding growth of a vine. To begin, place your right foot behind the left, then step sideways with your left foot. Cross your right foot in front of the left, and then take another step with your left foot. Keep alternating the movement of your right foot behind, then in front of your left as you step with your left.

After the energy has reached its peak and you have released it, bring your dancing to an end. Stop the tape or CD. Take a few minutes to ground your energy.

Closing

Walk to the edge of the circle in the respective direction as you dismiss each. After speaking, extinguish a candle on the altar. Stand in front of the altar when addressing the Goddess and God.

Speak   Lady, Goddess of All, thank you for the gifts you bestow on me and for joining my circle this night. I ask for your blessing as you depart, and bid you farewell.

Lord, God of All, thank you for the gifts you bestow on me and for joining my circle this night. I ask for your blessing as you depart, and bid you farewell.

Spirits of west, of water, thank you for the gift of dreams and self-discovery. I ask for your blessing as you depart, and bid you farewell.

Spirits of south, of fire, thank you for the gift of transformation. I ask for your blessing as you depart, and bid you farewell.

Spirits of east, of air, thank you for the gift of nature's voice. I ask for your blessing as you depart, and bid you farewell.

Spirits of north, of earth, thank you for the gift of connection with sacred places. I ask for your blessing as you depart, and bid you farewell.

Standing in front of your altar, say:

> In sacred circle's fading light,
> Through the stillness of this night.
> Intended gifts, fly from me,
> To those I named, so mote it be.
> In faith and unity, blessed be.

MOON BEFORE THE DARK

October

A mild breeze whispers on sunny afternoons, but night comes earlier as the harbingers of winter steal leaves from the trees. Moonlight shimmers on the first wet frost as earth prepares for sleep. In the Celtic tree month of ivy, this powerful evergreen teaches us about strength and endurance, death and immortality. Ivy is a symbol of the knowledge of things that are hidden and mysterious. The dark of the year is a time for us to enter the darkness in ourselves. Learn from ivy and find what is hidden within you.

Other Names for This Moon

- Blood Moon

- Hunter's Moon

- Harvest Moon

In the Celtic Tree Calendar

October 1–27: Ivy—associated with resurrection, transformation, and reflection.

October 28–31: Reed—associated with health and healing, knowledge and learning, and one's unfolding destiny.

Themes

- Experience the work of J. R. R. Tolkien as story comes to life.

- Enjoy the magic and wonder of story and myth.

Story for This Ritual

For both solo and group rituals, a place has been indicated where to read the following:

This is the Moon Before the Dark, but tonight we call it *Isilnarquelië*, the Moon of October. *Narquelië* is an enchanting month. It is especially magic as we approach All Hallows. It is a time of dark evenings. The air is crisp and leaves crunch underfoot. Bare tree branches reach like silver hands toward *Isil*, the moon.

At this time of year we begin to draw closer to home as darkness enfolds us earlier each day. In times past when the harvest was finished, evenings were a time to gather with family and friends and listen to stories. Around the "tale fires," myths and legends would be shared. The gods, goddesses, and ancient heroes would come to life.

This is a story of how the world was formed and how the sun and the moon came into existence, according to J. R. R. Tolkien. The world itself was sung into existence by the music of Ainur; you can think of them as angels. The Ainur's choir of beautiful voices singing exquisite harmonies was combined with the spark, "the secret fire that burns at the heart of the world,"[1] which was provided by the gods. A soft light of white and gold lit this new-formed place. The "great ones," called the Valar, entered the new world. One of the four great ones was Manwë. His wife Varda, "Queen of the Stars," was also among them. Others included Yavanna and her younger sister Vána.

This point in time was called *Lomendánar*—"the Days of Gloaming." Even though the world was lit with silver and gold light, the light was not "gathered together" and so the world seemed always in twilight. To concentrate the light and make it stronger, two mighty lamps were raised upon great pillars. One lamp shed light of silver and the other of gold.

Another of the great ones called Melko (also known as Melkor and Morgoth) declared that the pillars were strong and would last for all time. However, he knew that the pillars were actually made of ice. Melko was the original Dark Lord who later became the mentor of Sauron.

The lamps upon the pillars blazed and lit the world, but their heat soon began to melt the ice. As the pillars thawed, the seas rose. Eventually, the falling flame of the lamps created fires upon the land. The world fell into gloaming again.

The Valar moved west to the Outerlands and built mighty mountains around the land that became known as Valinor. In the middle of their land they dug two pits. In one they placed seven gold rocks from the sea and a fragment of the broken lamp of golden light. In the other pit they placed three large pearls and a star provided by Varda. Rich earth was used to cover each pit and then songs were sung around the newly created mounds.

After a time, a small shoot emerged from one of the pits. It began to glow with a soft yellow light. As it grew, golden buds emerged and then leaves of dark green with golden light around their edges. Gold flowers hung in clusters and blazed like bright lamps that gave illumination to the world. This tree was named Laurelin.

After twelve hours of light from Laurelin a shoot arose from the other mound. It shed a soft silver light. As it grew, its bark was like a white pearl. Blue-green, spear-shaped leaves sprouted, followed by great flowers that blossomed and spilled radiant silver light across the land. Its light was not as bright as Laurelin's. This tree was named Silpion.

The trees didn't have sap as we know trees to have. Instead their sap was light, and so each was "watered" with the light of the other.

As Silpion's silver light grew in strength, the light of Laurelin faded. And so the cycle began: As Silpion's light grew, Laurelin's faded, and then as Laurelin's grew, Silpion's faded. Laurelin's bright golden light created day and Silpion's luminescence softened the darkness. In between times, during the fading and growing of light, a delicate mingling of gold and silver created a soft twilight.

And so for several thousand years there was peace and beauty in Valinor. This was the time when the firstborn, the Elves, were awakened and brought into the world.

But the mountains that surrounded Valinor did not keep Melko out. He hated the rekindled light and plotted to destroy the trees just as he had the two lamps. Forming an alliance with the great horrible spider, Ungoliont, they crept into Valinor during a festival and attacked and devastated the trees. Once again, the world fell into darkness.

The Valar were grieved that their trees of wonder had been destroyed. Gathering all the gold they could find, they "watered" Laurelin with all their wealth. Yavanna brought phials of gold and silver, stood between the two trees, and cast down the vessels in an attempt to revive them, but to no avail.

The Valar went to their homes but Vána stayed behind. As she wept upon Laurelin, she wrapped her long blond braid around the tree stump. A small shoot appeared from the blackened tree.

"*I-Kal'anúlién*. Light hath returned,"[2] she shouted and the other Valar returned.

Blooms appeared on this new shoot, but a wind blew the petals from the tree. One radiant flower remained and produced a fruit. Vána said to cut it from the tree, but others disagreed. Before anything could be decided, the fruit fell to the ground. As it broke open, a dazzling light like red and amber flames shot skyward. The Valar called upon the gods to build a ship and launch the brilliant light into the heavens beyond Melko's reach. As it rose in the sky, the heavens turned from black to blue.

Lórien, one of the Lords of the Valar, sat beside Silpion and sang. As had happened with Laurelin, a small shoot appeared, followed by a few dark green leaves. As the leaves grew, one flower appeared and was called the "Rose of Silpion." Before the flower could fully open, the bough broke and crashed to the ground, bruising the rose.

Lórien called on the gods to create another ship with which to launch the Rose of Silpion into the heavens. A boat of clear Elfin glass was made to hold the rose. The Ship of the Moon was sent into the sky and eventually, like the dance of light between Laurelin and Silpion, the courses of the sun and moon were set.

Now, when you look upon the sun as it crosses the sky and when you see the moon's mysterious sheen, think of Valinor. Remember the two trees, the beauty and the peace that once existed.

Preparation

Items needed for this ritual include the following:

- Six candles, one of which should be silver and one gold

- Pictures, trinkets, or any memorabilia from J. R. R. Tolkien's work to decorate the altar (optional)

- Tape deck for solo practitioners who may want to tape the story and play it back (optional)

Group Ritual

Casting the Circle

Priestess   Tonight we pay tribute to the writer J. R. R. Tolkien for all the magic and wonder he has brought to our world. Tonight we cast a circle that draws us to Middle-earth, that connects us to Valinor in the days before the Silmarils. These were the days lit by the gentle light of the two trees.

Hand to hand the circle is cast.

The Priestess takes the hand of the person on her left. Each person in turn repeats the phrase around the circle. When everyone has joined hands, the Priestess says:

By the holy Faeries and immortal Elves, our circle is cast. We have created sacred space in a realm beyond our own.

Calling the Quarters

Each participant walks to the edge of the circle in their respective direction, then lights a candle on the altar after speaking. The Priest and Priestess stand in front of the altar.

North   We call to *Formen*, the north, and its power and strength. We call to the Dwarves, Durin's folk, masters of metalcraft. Join us in our circle. *Aiya.*

All   *Aiya.*

East   We call to *Rómen*, the east, and its glory. We call to the Elves, the Eldar who bring learning and beauty to Middle-earth. Join us in our circle. *Aiya.*

All	*Aiya.*
South	We call to *Hyarmen,* the south, and its untrodden wilds. We call to the Hobbits, people of the Shire with joyful spirits. Join us in our circle. *Aiya.*
All	*Aiya.*
West	We call to *Númen,* the west, and its mysteries. We call to the Vanyar, first and smallest of Tol Eressëa across the western sea. Join us in our circle. *Aiya.*
All	*Aiya.*
Priest	We call to *Ilyaheru,* Lord of All. Come to us as Laurelin, the Golden Tree and source of the sun. *Aiya.*
All	*Aiya.*
Priestess	We call to *Ilyatári,* Lady of All. Come to us as Silpion, the White Tree and source of the moon. *Aiya.*
All	*Aiya.*

Story for This Ritual

Invite people to get comfortable. The Priestess and Priest may want to take turns reading parts of the story.

Priestess	And now it is time to end our story and move back to our own realm.

Closing

After speaking, each participant, in turn, puts out the candle he or she lit at the beginning of the ritual.

Priestess	*Ilyatári,* Lady of All, thank you for the beauty and mystery of moonsheen. We will carry in our hearts the memory of Silpion, the White Tree. We bid you farewell. *Laita.*
All	*Laita,* Lady of All.

Priest	*Ilyaheru*, Lord of All, thank you for the beauty and radiance of the sun. We will carry in our hearts the memory of Laurelin, the Golden Tree. We bid you farewell. *Laita.*

All	*Laita*, Lord of All.

West	*Númen*, west, holy Vanyar, thank you for your presence this night. We bid you farewell as we return to our own realm. *Laita.*

All	*Laita*, Vanyar.

South	*Hyarmen*, south, dear Hobbits, thank you for your presence this night. We bid you farewell as we return to our own realm. *Laita.*

All	*Laita*, Hobbits.

East	*Rómen*, east, blessed Elves, thank you for your presence this night. We bid you farewell as we return to our own realm. *Laita.*

All	*Laita*, Elves.

North	*Formen*, north, stalwart Dwarves, thank you for your presence this night. We bid you farewell as we return to our own realm. *Laita.*

All	*Laita*, Dwarves.

Everyone joins hands.

Priestess	We have joined in the magic of myth this night as people have done for millennia. We pay tribute to Tolkien for the wonder and beauty he has given our world.

All	Merry meet, merry part, and merry meet again. *Laita.*

Solo Ritual

Casting the Circle

As you walk the perimeter of your circle say:

Isilnarquelië, Moon Before the Dark,
To the realm of Middle-earth, this night I mark,
Remembering the light of the two trees,
By the Holy Faeries, sacred space I decree.

Calling the Quarters

Walk to the edge of the circle in each direction and speak, then light its corresponding candle on the altar. Stand in front of the altar for the Goddess and God.

Speak   I call to *Formen,* the north, and its power and strength. I call to the Dwarves, Durin's folk, masters of metalcraft. Join me in my circle. *Aiya.*

I call to *Rómen,* the east, and its glory. I call to the Elves, the Eldar who bring learning and beauty to Middle-earth. Join me in my circle. *Aiya.*

I call to *Hyarmen,* the south, and its untrodden wilds. I call to the Hobbits, people of the Shire with joyful spirits. Join me in my circle. *Aiya.*

I call to *Númen,* the west, and its mysteries. I call to the Vanyar, first and smallest of Tol Eressëa across the western sea. Join me in my circle. *Aiya.*

I call to *Ilyaheru,* Lord of All. Come, be with me as Laurelin, the Golden Tree and source of the sun. *Aiya.*

I call to *Ilyatári,* Lady of All. Come, be with me as Silpion, the White Tree and source of the moon. *Aiya.*

Story for This Ritual

If you did not tape the story, you may want to read it aloud and enjoy the magic of storytelling.

Closing

After speaking, extinguish the candles in reverse order from which they were lit.

Speak   *Ilyatári,* Lady of All, thank you for the beauty and mystery of moonsheen. I will carry in my heart the memory of Silpion, the White Tree. I bid you farewell. *Laita.*

Ilyaheru, Lord of All, thank you for the beauty and radiance of the sun. I will carry in my heart the memory of Laurelin, the Golden Tree. I bid you farewell. *Laita.*

Númen, west, holy Vanyar, thank you for your presence this night. I bid you farewell as I return to my own realm. *Laita.*

Hyarmen, south, dear Hobbits, thank you for your presence this night. I bid you farewell as I return to my own realm. *Laita.*

Rómen, east, blessed Elves, thank you for your presence this night. I bid you farewell as I return to my own realm. *Laita.*

Formen, north, stalwart Dwarves, thank you for your presence this night. I bid you farewell as I return to my own realm. *Laita.*

Facing the altar, say:

My circle is open but unbroken,
No longer sacred, this space I decree.
Words of wonder have been spoken,
In faith and unity, blessed be.
Laita.

---

1. J. R. R. Tolkien, *The Book of Lost Tales 1* (New York: Ballantine Publishing Group, 1983), 53.
2. Ibid., 206.

MOON OF DESCENT

November

November is a time that is betwixt and between as we move further into the dark of the year. After confronting our own mortality at Samhain, November is a time to turn inward and examine the truths (and falsehoods) in our lives to enable us to move forward and grow.

Other Names for This Moon

- Snow Moon

- Mourning Moon

- Frosty Moon

In the Celtic Tree Calendar

November 1–24: Reed—associated with health/healing, overindulgence, and wounds.

November 25–30: Elder—associated with purification, divination, problem solving; this is the tree of life and death and prophecy.

Themes

- Prepare for the dark months ahead.

- Take a shamanic journey to the underworld.

Meditation for This Ritual

A place has been indicated in the ritual for this meditation. Solo practitioners will want to record this and play it back. For group ritual the Priestess and Priest may want to take turns reading the meditation while the other softly drums. Appropriate music can also be played:

We have entered the dark of the year. Days grow cold and nights long. The earth begins her winter's rest. The Crone beckons: "Come into the darkness, explore what lies within."

November is a time that is betwixt and between. We have passed through the gateway of Samhain into the dark of the year, and we await the rebirth of light, the rebirth of the Lord at Yule. This moon, the Moon of Descent, gives us the opportunity to descend within ourselves and find the inner realm. It is through this inner place that we can connect with other realms. Tonight we are going to visit our inner realm.

Close your eyes and get comfortable. Become aware of your feet on the floor. Feel your energy move through your feet, down through the floor, down through this building directly to the earth. Feel Mother Earth's energy join with your energy. Your body may feel heavy as it becomes grounded.

Now, draw the energy up through your body. Feel the vital lifeforce move through you. As you feel this movement, become aware that you are walking through the woods. Leaves blanket the ground and the air is crisp. You walk along a path that follows a small ridge overlooking a slow-moving river. The path splits to skirt around two trees that grow in the middle of the path. These trees are about four feet apart. These are the gateway trees.

Stop in between these trees, raise your hands to shoulder height and place one of your palms on each tree. Say to yourself, "And so, I enter." Feel the energy of the trees move through you. When you are ready, move onward.

The path curves to the left, but you continue forward. You see that the ground slopes into a small valley where a stream trickles down a little stepped waterfall. You move forward down the steep slope where bare rock provides rugged steps. As you climb down you notice a large gnarled oak tree growing from the rock. This is the Merlin tree that guards this enchanted valley. You begin to feel the energy of land.

The only sound is the trickling water farther down the slope. When you reach level ground beside the Merlin tree, you turn to your left. The ground below the path you left before climbing down forms a right angle that towers twenty feet above you. Where the rock and earth is cleanly sheared away, a few small ferns have taken root. A narrow alcove in the rock wall is the size of a small door.

Soften your gaze and look at this rock wall. Part of it opens inward like a door. You enter and follow the path. There is a wall on your right, but the left seems to slope away, and even though you cannot see where it goes, you are not fearful of falling. There is a soft light from the rock above; just enough to allow you to see the path. Even though it is autumn, this underground route is not cold. It is as if the earth itself is providing warmth.

Ahead you hear voices. You cannot discern what is being said, but the voices sound friendly. As you draw near, you find that you are on a balcony overlooking a cavern. It is a great hall set with long tables. There are other beings below talking in groups. There is lively music.

To your left is a staircase that leads down to the floor of the hall. As you descend, a few of the beings notice you, but go back to their conversations. Despite being in a different place, you do not feel intimidated and you begin to walk through the hall. There is an empty bench at the other end. You walk toward it and have a seat. From here you can listen to the music and watch the others. What you hear and see may hold messages for you—things that may guide you through the dark of the year.

As you enjoy the music, one of the beings may come and sit beside you. You may ask questions, but do not demand answers. Even if a being does not speak with you directly, conversation that you overhear may hold information for you. Listen and feel the warmth of the energy that surrounds you. If you are compelled to walk around this great hall, do so.

Pause for approximately ten to fifteen minutes. This can be in silence or music can be inserted.

It is time to begin your return journey. If you have been speaking with one of the beings, thank them for their gift of wisdom. In return, offer them a gift. It may be a piece of jewelry that you wear, something in your pocket, or a piece of your clothing. Give something that has value to you and give it freely. Once you climb the stairs to the balcony you may want to pause a moment and look at the hall. Does it seem different from when you entered?

Retrace your route along the dim passage, then through the doorway where you find yourself standing next to the wall of rock below the Merlin tree. Instead of climbing back up to the path in the woods, walk further down the slope to the stream and tiny waterfall. There are small pools along the steps between each small fall of water. The little valley pulses with magic energy and it makes you smile because you haven't felt this close to the web of life since you were a child. Dip your hand in the silvery reflection of a pool and thank the beings below in the underworld.

It is time to return to your own world. Climb up the slope, using the roots of the Merlin tree to steady you. Find the path and follow it. At the gateway trees in the middle of the path, pause again. Place a palm on each tree and say to yourself: "And so I leave, to return again."

The forest around you begins to fade. Become aware of this room. Feel your feet on the floor. Become aware of your energy and the earth energy that has been holding you. Let excess energy flow to Mother Earth as you return to your everyday consciousness. When you are ready, open your eyes.

Preparation

Items needed for this ritual include the following:

- Black altar cloth

- Five black candles

- A crystal ball or round scrying mirror

- Acorns or hazelnuts, enough for each participant

- A small bell for solo ritual

Except for these things, the altar should be bare.

Group Ritual

Casting the Circle

Taking the crystal ball (or scrying mirror) from the altar, the Priestess holds it in the palm of her hand (or in both hands depending on the size) and walking around the outside of the gathered circle says:

Under the soft gaze of Luna, we pass to another realm.
This night we pass to the realm of the underworld.

When she returns to her place, and before placing the ball back on the altar, she says:
The circle is cast. We have passed through the gateway between the worlds.

Calling the Quarters

Going to the edge of the circle in his or her respective direction, each participant speaks and then lights a candle. The Priestess stands before the altar.

North	In your quiet caverns, deep places of the underworld, we beckon to the spirits of north, of earth, to join us in our circle this dark night.
All	Join us in our circle this dark night.
East	With soft breath and still air of silent places, we beckon to the spirits of east, of air, to join us in our circle this dark night.
All	Join us in our circle this dark night.
South	With a single candle, small flame that casts a soft light, we beckon to the spirits of south, of fire, to join us in our circle this dark night.
All	Join us in our circle this dark night.
West	There is a small trickle that seeps below the surface. We beckon to the spirits of west, of water, to join us in our circle this dark night.
All	Join us in our circle this dark night.
Priestess	Sister Luna, your pale sheen prompts us to be quiet, to be still, to listen. We beckon to you, join us in our circle this dark night.
All	Join us in our circle this dark night.

Meditation

Invite participants to get comfortable, and then read the meditation.

The Priestess or a helper goes around the circle and places an acorn or hazelnut in the hand of each participant.

Priest   Receive this gift from the forest. Remember the beings you met and saw in the underworld. Know that your journey there gave depth to your inner journey. Know that your inner world touches other realms.

Closing

After speaking, each participant extinguishes the candle he or she lit.

Priestess   The pale light within the earth is mirrored by the soft light of the moon. Sister Luna, we thank you for standing guard on our journey and for your presence this night. Stay if you will, go if you must. We bid you farewell.

All   We bid you farewell.

West   From your enchanted streams and underground pools, spirits of the west, of water, thank you for your presence this night. Stay if you will, go if you must. We bid you farewell.

All   We bid you farewell.

South   From your soft light that shines within the earth, spirits of the south, of fire, thank you for your presence this night. Stay if you will, go if you must. We bid you farewell.

All   We bid you farewell.

East   From your gentle air that follows the paths and fills the caverns of earth, spirits of the east, of air, thank you for your presence this night. Stay if you will, go if you must. We bid you farewell.

All   We bid you farewell.

North   From your quiet places, magical places that hold knowledge and wisdom from the deep realms, spirits of the north, of earth, thank you for your presence this night. Stay if you will, go if you must. We bid you farewell.

All   We bid you farewell.

Everyone joins hands.

Priestess	A journey within brings us deeper inside ourselves and deeper into the flow of the other realms. In the days ahead think of the beings you saw and met, and what you heard on your journey this night. When you touch others with your energy you touch more than you can see. Take comfort in what you have learned.
All	Merry meet, merry part, and merry meet again. Blessed be.

Solo Ritual

Casting the Circle

Take the crystal ball (or scrying mirror) from the altar and walk around the perimeter of your circle saying:

> Crystal sphere, the shape of Luna,
> Deep your secrets lie within.
> May I find the path to follow
> For now 'tis time to begin.

When you return to where you started, say:
The circle is cast. I have passed through the gateway between the worlds.

Calling the Quarters

Go to the edge of the circle in each direction to speak and then light a candle. For the Goddess, stand before the altar.

Speak	In your quiet caverns, deep places of the underworld, I beckon to the spirits of north, of earth, to join me in my circle this dark night.
	With soft breath and still air of silent places, I beckon to the spirits of east, of air, to join me in my circle this dark night.
	With a single candle, small flame that casts a soft light, I beckon to the spirits of south, of fire, to join me in my circle this dark night.

There is a small trickle that seeps below the surface. I beckon to the spirits of west, of water, to join me in my circle this dark night.

Sister Luna, your pale sheen prompts me to be quiet, to be still, to listen. I beckon to you, join me in my circle this dark night.

Meditation

Play back the recorded meditation.

Take an acorn or hazelnut from the altar and close your hand over it. Think of it as a gift from the forest, and remember the beings you met and saw in the underworld. Know that your journey there gave depth to your inner journey. Know that your inner world touches other realms.

Closing

After speaking, extinguish the candles in the opposite order in which they were lit.

Speak   The pale light within the earth is mirrored by the soft light of the moon. Sister Luna, I thank you for standing guard on my journey and for your presence this night. Stay if you will, go if you must. I bid you farewell.

From your enchanted streams and underground pools, spirits of the west, of water, thank you for your presence this night. Stay if you will, go if you must. I bid you farewell.

From your soft light that shines within the earth, spirits of the south, of fire, thank you for your presence this night. Stay if you will, go if you must. I bid you farewell.

From your gentle air that follows the paths and fills the caverns of earth, spirits of the east, of air, thank you for your presence this night. Stay if you will, go if you must. I bid you farewell.

From your quiet places, magical places that hold knowledge and wisdom from the deep realms, spirits of the north, of earth, thank you for your presence this night. Stay if you will, go if you must. I bid you farewell.

Ring the bell gently three times, and then say:

In faith and in unity with other realms, blessed be.

MOON OF COMPLETION

December

A s the year draws to a close and holiday preparations become a frenzied blur, pause in the moonlight and step out of that frazzled mindset to take a look at your life. Note whether or not you have moved toward your personal and spiritual goals. It is not so important that you have reached these goals as long as you are working in the direction you want to go. Know that you cannot change what has passed but you can chart your course for what is to be.

Other Names for This Moon

- Oak Moon (if it falls before the winter solstice)

- Cold Moon

- Snow Moon

In the Celtic Tree Calendar

December 1–22: Elder—associated with prophecy and seeing beyond what is on the surface.

December 23 is the proverbial day in the "year and a day" and does not have a tree associated with it.

December 24–31: Birch—associated with new beginnings, changes, and quiet determination.

Background for This Ritual

A place has been indicated in both the solo and group rituals where this is most appropriate to read:

> Moonlight glitters on the frosty earth. Time seems frozen, but the night air tingles with energy. This is the Moon of Completion. We have come full circle through the twelve months. As the Wheel of the Year makes its final turn and begins a new cycle, we pause to reflect on the path that brought us here and where it may lead us in the year to come.
>
> Through ritual we focus our minds and energy on intention. Stating an intention is the first step in manifesting what you want into the physical realm. Stating intention is a sacred process and a magical act when it is invested with your heart and soul.
>
> A tree symbolizes many things. The Tree of Life connects the realms. It also symbolizes unity. Like the branches of a tree, you bring many aspects of your life together in your spirituality. Tonight a branch is a symbol for unity and intention.

Themes

- Reaffirm your spirituality.

- State your intentions and commitments for the year ahead.

Preparation

This is planned as an outdoor ritual with a bonfire. If this is not possible, plan to burn, bury, or somehow commit back to nature the things used. Items needed for this ritual include the following:

- A tree branch with a number of smaller branches of a size depending on the size of the group and whether or not you are outdoors around a bonfire

- Basket of ribbons or yarn cut to twelve-inch lengths, or shorter if you are using a small branch

- Drums (optional)

Group Ritual

Casting the Circle

Priestess We come together in community and give our names. I am _____.

As the Priestess says her name, she raises the tree branch and then passes it to the person on her left. Each person in turn states his or her name and passes the branch. When it is returned to the Priestess, she places it on the ground near the bonfire and says:

> The circle is cast. We come together as people of strong purpose to complete this year.

Calling the Quarters

Each participant faces his or her respective direction from the opposite side of the circle. The Priest and Priestess stand near the bonfire.

North Spirits of north, of earth, we call to you this night. Be with us as the quiet meadows wrapped in a blanket of welcoming snow. We bid you welcome to our circle.

All We bid you welcome.

East Spirits of east, of air, we call to you this night. Be with us as the soft whisper that is heard in the frozen stillness of the woods. We bid you welcome to our circle.

All We bid you welcome.

South Spirits of south, of fire, we call to you this night. Be with us as the pale sunlight that softly illuminates but does not disturb the sleepers. We bid you welcome to our circle.

All We bid you welcome.

West Spirits of west, of water, we call to you this night. Be with us as the clear ice that holds nature's secrets until the spring. We bid you welcome to our circle.

All We bid you welcome.

Priest   Lord of All, we call to you this night. Be with us as the vital spark that rests quietly within the world, within the womb. We bid you welcome to our circle.

All   We bid you welcome.

Priestess   Lady of All, we call to you this night. Be with us as the slumbering Goddess who renews the world through a long peaceful sleep. We bid you welcome to our circle.

All   We bid you welcome.

Priestess   We have joined together as a community for a year. We have shared in each other's lives, given and received support, and joined together in sacred ritual. Tonight it is time to look ahead to our collective future. Think of your intentions for being here. Why are you in the group? What do you seek? What would you like to find here? Tonight we invite you to share your intentions and personal commitments you would like to make to the group, as well as commitments you feel we should make as a group.

Background

Share the background information here.

    Picking up the branch, the Priest says:

Like these branches, we bring many things to the group and join as one. Tonight we will use this as we make our intentions known. When you are ready, come forward and take a piece of ribbon from the basket. Hold it between your hands as you think of your intention. Invest it with your love. Then as you state your intention to the group, tie the ribbon to one of the branches. Your intention may be that you have come to build community, to learn and share your spirituality. Whatever it is, know that you have a voice here.

The Priest holds the branch as people come forward. The Priestess may drum or hum to gently stir the energy, however, the sound should be soft enough to allow people's voices to be heard. After participants have stated their intentions, the Priestess states hers, and then holds the branch for the Priest.

Holding the branch high above her head, the Priestess walks around the circle and says:

> We have come together as people of strong purpose. We have made our intentions and commitments known this night.

After a complete circuit, the Priestess hands the branch to the Priest who holds it over the flame of the bonfire. As it begins to catch, he gently lowers it into the fire and says:

> As the sacred fire consumes this branch, our intentions are released to transform into energy, which will work to manifest them into the physical world.

The Priestess begins a chant and circle dance around the fire:

> Come into the circle, join us here.
> Singing, dancing, share our cheer.
> Stating our intentions loud and clear.
> Stirring up magic at end of year.

After the energy has reached its peak, the Priest and Priestess slow, then stop the chanting and dancing.

Priestess   As the fire dwindles and its energy unwinds, so, too, shall ours. Take a deep breath and close your eyes. Become aware of your feet on solid ground, directly touching Mother Earth. Let your extra energy flow to her. Let her balance bring you to center. When you are ready, open your eyes.

Closing

Each participant faces his or her direction from the opposite side of the circle. The Priest and Priestess face the bonfire.

Priestess   Lady of All, you have come to us this night and witnessed our intentions. We ask for your blessings as we complete this year and prepare to move on to the next. Thank you for your presence with us this night. Stay if you will, go if you must. We bid you farewell.

All   We bid you farewell.

Priest   Lord of All, you have come to us this night and witnessed our intentions. We ask for your blessings as we complete this year and prepare to move

	on to the next. Thank you for your presence with us this night. Stay if you will, go if you must. We bid you farewell.
All	We bid you farewell.
West	Spirits of west, of water, may your clear ice that holds nature's secrets also hold our intentions. Thank you for your presence with us this night. Stay if you will, go if you must. We bid you farewell.
All	We bid you farewell.
South	Spirits of south, of fire, may the pale winter sun illuminate our intentions. Thank you for your presence with us this night. Stay if you will, go if you must. We bid you farewell.
All	We bid you farewell.
East	Spirits of east, of air, may the crisp air whisper our intentions through the winter. Thank you for your presence with us this night. Stay if you will, go if you must. We bid you farewell.
All	We bid you farewell.
North	Spirits of north, of earth, may your meadows receive our intentions and help them grow in the spring. Thank you for your presence with us this night. Stay if you will, go if you must. We bid you farewell.
All	We bid you farewell.

Everyone joins hands.

Priestess

As all good things must sometimes end,
Go forth with the love the Goddess sends.
For if your heart is always true,
This circle will come back to you.

All   Merry meet, merry part, and merry meet again.

Solo Ritual

Casting the Circle

Walk around the perimeter of your circle carrying the branch as you say:

> This circle I cast at year's finish,
> Faith and unity never diminish.
> Sacred this space I now decree,
> As above, so below, so mote it be.

Calling the Quarters

Face each direction as you speak. For the Lord and Lady, face center.

Speak   Spirits of north, of earth, I call to you this night. Be with me as the quiet meadows wrapped in a blanket of welcoming snow. I bid you welcome to my circle.

Spirits of east, of air, I call to you this night. Be with me as the soft whisper that is heard in the frozen stillness of the woods. I bid you welcome to my circle.

Spirits of south, of fire, I call to you this night. Be with me as the pale sunlight that softly illuminates but does not disturb the sleepers. I bid you welcome to my circle.

Spirits of west, of water, I call to you this night. Be with me as the clear ice that holds nature's secrets until the spring. I bid you welcome to my circle.

Lord of All, I call to you this night. Be with me as the vital spark that rests quietly within the world, within the womb. I bid you welcome to my circle.

Lady of All, I call to you this night. Be with me as the slumbering Goddess who renews the world through a long peaceful sleep. I bid you welcome to my circle.

Background

Read the background material here.

Think of your intentions for doing ritual. Why are you following this path? What do you seek? What would you like to find in your spiritual life? What commitments or renewal of commitments do you want to make to your spirituality? Tonight give voice to your intentions and commitments.

Take a piece of ribbon from the basket. Hold it between your hands as you think of your intention. Invest it with your love. As you state your intention, tie the ribbon to one of the branches. It may be that you want to deepen your spirituality or seek other ways to express it. Use a separate ribbon for each intention/commitment.

When you are finished, hold the branch high above your head and walk around the circle saying:

> I have come here this night with strong purpose. I have made my intentions and commitments known.

Lower the branch over the fire or set it alight safely in your cauldron, and say:

> As the sacred fire consumes this branch, my intentions are released to transform into energy, which will work to manifest them into the physical world.

As the branch burns, begin a chant as you dance around the fire or cauldron:

> Moving like a wheel, I circle here.
> Singing, dancing in good cheer.
> Stating my intentions loud and clear.
> Stirring up magic at end of year.

When it feels appropriate, bring your chanting and movement to stillness. Use your usual method for grounding energy.

Closing

Face each direction as you speak; turn to center for the Lord and Lady.

Speak   Lady of All, you have come to me this night and witnessed my intentions. I ask for your blessings as I complete this year and prepare to move on to the next. Thank you for your presence with me this night. Stay if you will, go if you must. I bid you farewell.

Lord of All, you have come to me this night and witnessed my intentions. I ask for your blessings as I complete this year and prepare to move on to the next. Thank you for your presence with me this night. Stay if you will, go if you must. I bid you farewell.

Spirits of west, of water, may your clear ice that holds nature's secrets also hold my intentions. Thank you for your presence with me this night. Stay if you will, go if you must. I bid you farewell.

Spirits of south, of fire, may the pale winter sun illuminate my intentions. Thank you for your presence with me this night. Stay if you will, go if you must. I bid you farewell.

Spirits of east, of air, may the crisp air whisper my intentions through the winter. Thank you for your presence with me this night. Stay if you will, go if you must. I bid you farewell.

Spirits of north, of earth, may your meadows receive my intentions and help them grow in the spring. Thank you for your presence with me this night. Stay if you will, go if you must. I bid you farewell.

Walk around your circle as you say:

Wheel of the Year, cycle complete.
Endings, beginnings, both shall meet.
What lies ahead, I cannot see.
My faith I will follow, blessed be.

APPENDIX A

Your Practice

Whether or not you celebrate all the sabbats and esbats is a personal matter. If you cannot observe it "on the day," try to do so beforehand as energy is building up to it. If you are pressed for time and cannot do a complete ritual, take a few minutes to light a candle, center yourself, and contemplate the sabbat or esbat. Think about what it means to you. Make it personal.

Use the rituals in this book as stepping stones to creating your own. Experiment and try different things. Take time to invest love in what you create and you will be rewarded with ripples of good energy.

Creating Your Own Rituals

Rituals have a basic format that can be as simple or intricate as you like. When working with a group, you may want to involve several people in creating a ritual to add richness and diversity. Following is a brief overview of ritual components.

Call to Worship

A call to worship is an optional component of group ritual that begins to focus attention as people make the transition from everyday awareness to sacred space. This can be done prior to leading participants through an energy exercise (see appendix E) if people are not used to preparing themselves for ritual. The call to worship is brief but sets the tone for the gathering. Many of the group rituals in this book include a call to worship as the first part of casting the circle.

Casting the Circle

A circle is cast to create sacred space and separate ourselves from everyday life. The circle is a boundary that provides protection from energy that is unwanted within the ritual. In keeping out the unwanted, it provides protection and allows participants to safely open themselves psychically to fully participate in ritual. The circle becomes a cauldron that holds our sacred energy until we are ready to release it. The circle is three-dimensional. It extends above and below us ("As above, so below") and connects the realms.

Casting the circle can be done by "drawing" it with athame, sword, or wand in the air or on the ground as the Priest, Priestess, or solo practitioner walks the perimeter. In group ritual it is the Priestess, Priest, or both who cast the circle. Alternatively, they can initiate and complete the casting, but involve all participants in creating the circle. The rituals in this book use the latter method. This is a matter of preference as is consecrating/cleansing the space either before the altar is set up or after the circle is cast.

Like all parts of ritual, casting the circle can be as simple or elaborate as you care to make it. Many of the rituals in this book include placing objects on the floor at the circle's boundary. This is not necessary as it is intention and energy that forms the circle, however, I find that the physical act of marking the circle helps to mentally establish it. Knowing where the boundary lies is useful in group ritual that includes dancing.

When working in groups, a gatekeeper is sometimes assigned to "cut" a doorway through the energy to allow people to pass into and out of the circle. This can also be left to individuals to do for themselves. Others believe that an entire room or a certain amount of space outdoors is made sacred and that passing in or out of the circle does not require a door to cut through the energy. Follow what feels appropriate.

Calling the Quarters and the Divine

Once the circle has been established, we acknowledge and call the quarters: the four directions and/or elements, which helps to align our energies with the natural world. Some traditions make a distinction between directions and elements; others do not. There are a variety of direction/element pairings, as well as the order in which they are called. As with all things concerned with your spiritual path, follow what is appropriate for you.

The elements and directions provide a measure of time because they are part of a cycle; they represent the "moods" of the earth's soul. The elements and directions are means through which the Divine relates with us. When we call upon the "spirit" of a direction or element for protection or to join our circle, we are evoking the energy embodied and represented by them. These energies are archetypal patterns for our energy and consciousness. Having all of the elements/directions present brings the circle and our energy into balance.

Last, and certainly not least, we call on the Divine to join our circle. The manner in which diverse traditions and solo practitioners view and interact with the Divine varies widely. Some traditions maintain certain names for the Goddess and God while others acknowledge them by various cultural or seasonal aspects. In the Dianic tradition, only the Goddess is called upon. The rituals in this book acknowledge both Goddess and God and call on them with different names, some according to season.

The basic action associated with calling the quarters and the Divine is lighting an altar candle. In addition, certain arm positions may be used (which everyone in a group may follow) or there are particular, and occasionally dramatic, positions in which the person doing the calling stands. These are a matter of tradition and/or preference.

Speaking roles are usually more poetic, sometimes archaic, and almost always grander than normal everyday language. Keep in mind that you have stepped out of your normal world and that you are addressing the Divine. However, it doesn't mean that the language you use needs to be uncomfortably weird. As long as your words are respectful and have meaning, they will be appropriate. I usually try to make these evocations (and the devocations) fit the theme and tone of the ritual so it flows evenly. Table 2 lists correspondences from various traditions. This is by no means a complete listing of all things that correspond to the elements, but it should give you a start in the right direction for creating the parts for your rituals.

The Core of a Ritual

Once everything—physically and energetically—has been set up, you are ready for the purpose of your ritual. Even though each sabbat has a standard purpose, how you celebrate it can be uniquely individual. The core purpose for esbats and other rituals are only limited by your imagination. Other components within the core part of the ritual can include:

TABLE 2
Table of Correspondences

ELEMENTS	EARTH	AIR	FIRE	WATER
Directions	North, east	East, north	South, west	West, south
Magical tools	Pentagram, stone	Athame, sword	Wand, spear, staff	Chalice, cauldron
Powers	To keep silence	To know	To will	To dare
Personal	The body	The mind	The spirit	The emotions
Seasons	Winter	Spring	Summer	Autumn
Times of day	Midnight	Dawn	Noon	Dusk
Colors	Green, black, brown	Yellow, red, light blue	Red, orange, gold, white	Blue, dark blue, green, gray
Elementals	Gnomes	Sylphs	Salamanders	Undines
Moon Phases	New/dark	Waxing	Full	Waning
Sabbats	Lughnasadh	Imbolg	Beltane	Samhain
Zodiac	Capricorn, Taurus, Virgo	Aquarius, Gemini, Libra	Aries, Leo, Sagittarius	Cancer, Pisces, Scorpio
Trees	Oak, ash, blackthorn	Aspen, apple, beech	Elder, gorse, hawthorn	Willow, alder, birch
Animals	Bear, bull, dog, snake, stage mouse, wolf	All birds, esp. the eagle, hawk, owl, dove	Lion, horse, bull, fox, ram lizards	All sea life, dolphins, turtles, swans
Basic attributes	Birth, growth, death, abundance, sustenance, foundation, connection	Knowledge, learning, intuition, inspiration, communication, creativity, truth	Healing, strength, destruction, purification, transformation, protection, personal power	Love, courage, inner wisdom, cleansing, release, receptivity, mystery, dreams

- **Cakes and Ale:** The actual food and drink can be anything although for sabbats you may want to keep them seasonal. Cakes and Ale are a way for a group to share the intimacy of "breaking bread" together and spiritually sustaining each other. The "Blessing of the Wine," which precedes Cakes and Ale, is usually symbolic of the Great Rite—the sexual union of Goddess and God, a balancing of female and male energies.

- **Spellwork:** Full moon rituals are frequently used for working spells (depending on the purpose of the spell). At minimum when doing a spell, a circle should be cast for protection and freedom in opening and working with your energy.

- **Chanting and dancing:** These activities are used to raise energy. In ritual it is important to disengage that chattering part of your mind and let your mind/body/spirit connect and flow as one. This facilitates the shift in consciousness. These activities also help to stir the cauldron of energy that puts power behind your ritual and any spellwork that may take place.

- **Drawing Down the Moon:** In esbats the Priestess and Priest may invoke the spirit of the Goddess and God, respectively, into themselves. This involves the Priest and Priestess allowing themselves to be open to receive the manifested energy of the Divine. Different traditions have various methods and means for accomplishing this. Others do not Draw Down the Moon. This is a matter of beliefs and how you personally interact with Divine energy.

Grounding

Before ending a ritual it is important to send excess energy to the ground. Energy raised in ritual is very strong and can become uncomfortable if you don't get rid of it. If you don't ground the extra energy you have absorbed, you may feel unsettled, spacey, restless, or disoriented, and after an evening ritual, you may not be able to sleep. Physically grounding energy also helps to bring your consciousness back to a level where you can function normally in the everyday world.

Closing

Winding down a ritual is done in the opposite order from which it was begun. The Goddess, God, and elementals are thanked for their presence and then basically told that they are free to stay or leave. The circle of energy is then dissolved and the space returned to its mundane plane of existence.

After ritual is a time for feasting and socializing. When working solo it can be a time for reflection and journaling.

Going Deeper

Observing the sabbats and esbats over time can bring a depth and fullness to your spirituality that will ripple into all parts of your life. Ritual provides a path through the unconscious into a deep well of possibility that is inside each of us. This is a spiral path that not only takes us deeper within, but also brings our true selves out. Tapping into this well of the self allows us to bring beauty and potential (that might otherwise lie dormant) to the surface of our lives.

Our everyday perspective begins to change as we increasingly experience a shift in consciousness during ritual. The mundane world starts to look different. For example, a tree is no longer just something sticking out of the ground. It is a living entity full of wisdom and beauty. As you go deeper, you'll discover that you can find peace and happiness within yourself and more meaningful relationships with others. As this happens, you'll find your place in the web of existence. Life is a journey in which your spiritual path can bring you beauty, wonder, and joy. Blessed be.

APPENDIX B

The Ogham

The origin of the ogham, also called the Celtic tree alphabet, is unknown; however, surviving samples are carved in stone and have been dated to approximately 300–600 CE.[1] The ogham consists of twenty characters called *feda* that are divided into four groups of five characters that connect to a center stem line. The stem line can be horizontal or vertical. Five other characters (*forfeda*) that represent diphthongs were added at a later time.

The ogham is believed to have been a bardic alphabet and that the letters could be represented by a tree, bird, or color. This system of symbols linked each letter to an array of concepts that held deep significance. While a complex study would be necessary to fully understand the ogham, we can tap into this rich resource by using them in ritual. Approach the ogham with respect and an open heart and you will begin to feel the energy and wisdom it contains.

The Ogham Stick

To create an ogham stick for use in ritual, select a branch as you would for making a wand. You may want to coordinate the type of wood with your purpose. For example, alder is associated with evolving spirit, hawthorn with spiritual energies, holly with guidance, and elder with divination. The types of trees in your area will also have a role in your choice.

TABLE 3
The Ogham Alphabet

LETTER	OGHAM	TREE	ASPECTS / ATTRIBUTES
B: Beth	⊥	Birch	Beginnings / Renewal / Changes
L: Luis	⊥⊥	Rowan	Insight / Blessings / Expression
F: Fearn	⊥⊥⊥	Alder	Solid foundation / Evolving spirit
S: Saille	⊥⊥⊥⊥	Willow	Intuition / Balance / Flexibility
N: Nion	⊥⊥⊥⊥⊥	Ash	Connections / Ambition / Enchantment
H: Uath	⊤	Hawthorn	Hope / Healing / Spiritual energies
D: Duir	⊤⊤	Oak	Self-confidence / Optimism / Strength
T: Tinne	⊤⊤⊤	Holly	Hearth and home / Unity / Guidance
C: Coll	⊤⊤⊤⊤	Hazel	Knowledge of secrets / Creativity / Justice
Q/CC: Quert	⊤⊤⊤⊤⊤	Apple	Rebirth / Love / Faithfulness
M: Muin	╱	Vine/Bramble	Opening and unlocking / Learning lessons
G: Gort	╱╱	Ivy	Growth / Love / Mystical / Transformation
Ng: Ngetal	╱╱╱	Reed	Health and healing / Knowledge / Destiny
Z/SS: Straif	╱╱╱╱	Blackthorn	Authority / Strength in adversity
R: Ruis	╱╱╱╱╱	Elder	Awareness / Change / Problem solving
A: Ailm	┼	Elm	Healing / Reaching / Rising above
O: Onn	┼┼	Gorse	Hope / Persistence
U: Ur	┼┼┼	Heather	Fresh perspective / Generosity
E: Eadha	┼┼┼┼	Aspen	Courage / Endurance / Communication
I: Idho	┼┼┼┼┼	Yew	Personal transformation

Note: This is not an exhaustive list of aspects and attributes.

Once you have chosen the type of wood and found a tree, look for branches that have already fallen. If you set your intention toward a particular tree, it may give you a gift of a branch. It is important to also be open to other trees that may present you with a branch. Try to find one that is reasonably straight and at least as long as the distance from your elbow to the tip of your middle finger. It needs to be thick enough to comfortably carve the ogham characters along one side.

Decide whether or not you want to remove the bark. If so, carefully peel it off with a sharp knife (an X-Acto knife works nicely) and avoid making nicks in the wood. If you leave the bark on, exposing light wood under dark bark makes the ogham more visible. If you remove the bark, once the characters are carved onto light wood you can use paint to make them darker. Alternatively, you could avoid carving altogether and just paint the ogham on the stick.

Measure how much space you need for your hand at the bottom end in order to hold the stick. Begin carving above this area to allow the entire ogham to be visible while you hold the stick. Begin by creating one line from the "handle" almost to the top of the stick. Using the drawing in Figure B1 as a guide, begin with the letter *B* just above the handle and work up toward the top. The ogham is read left to right or bottom to top. When written vertically, characters that are below the stem line are written to the right of this line. After you have finished, consecrate the stick with lavender or sandalwood oil and/or pass it through the smoke of frankincense, jasmine, or mugwort. Wrap it in a scarf or piece of cloth and put it away until you are ready to use it.

Celtic Tree Cards

Start with 3 x 5–inch index cards. Green ones are nice if you can find them or you may want to decorate white ones with pictures of trees or designs. The cards can remain full size or cut in half for smaller cards. On one side, draw the ogham character and print its name; on the other side put the tree name and attributes. See Figure B2.

---

1. David Allen Hulse, *The Western Mysteries* (St. Paul, MN: Llewellyn Publications, 2000), 107.

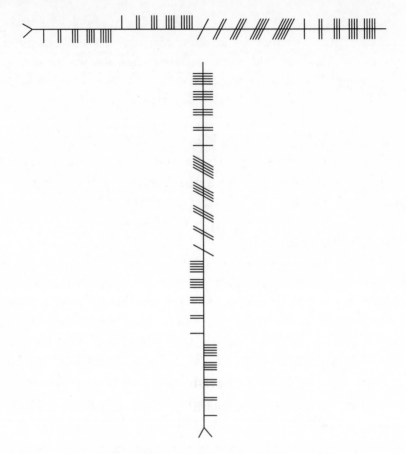

Figure B1—The ogham (horizontal and vertical)

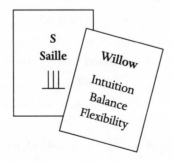

Figure B2—The Celtic tree cards

APPENDIX C

Glossary and Pronunciation Guide to Non-English Words

Elvish

Tolkien's books include pronunciation guidelines for Elvish, and there are many websites offering information. Included here is a quick guide to pronouncing the words used in the October moon ritual. Whenever possible, roll the *r*'s. An *h* at the beginning of a word has a breathy sound as in the word *huge*.

Ainur (*I noor*): Angels/angelic spirits.

Aiya (*I ya*): As a greeting "hail."

Durin: There were a series of great Dwarf kings named Durin who built the great underground palace of Khazad-dûm, later called the Mines of Moria.

Eldar: Encompasses the three kindred of Elves: Vanyar, Noldor, and Teleri.

Formen: North.

Hyarmen (*haar men*): East.

I-Kal'anúlién (*I kal annoo lee an*): "Light hath returned."

Ilyaheru (*eelya heroo*): Lord of All.

Ilyatári (*eelya taaree*): Queen (Lady) of All.

Isil (*ee-sil*): The moon.

Isilnarquelië (*ee-sil nar qwel ee ay*): Moon of October.

Laita (*lie ta*): Bless / praise.

Laurelin: The golden tree.

Lomendánar (*lo men da nar*): "Days of Gloaming"; the twilight time before light was "gathered" into the radiance of the two trees.

Lórien (*lo ree an*): One of the Lords of the Valar; also known as Irmo.

Manwë (*man way*): One of the eight chiefs of the Valar.

Melko: One of the wise and gifted Ainur who was impatient and jealous and turned against the others; he later became the mentor of Sauron; he is also known as Melkor and Morgoth.

Númen (*noo men*): South.

Rómen (*hroe men*): East.

Silmarils (*seel mar ills*): The three brilliant gems that shone with the light of the two trees.

Silpion (*seel pee on*): The white tree; also called Telperion.

Tol Eressëa (*tahl eres see aa*): An island off the coast of Valinor that enjoyed the light of the two trees; also called the Lonely Isle and the Lost Isle.

Ungoliont (*oon gah lee ahnt*): A giant spider that embodied the "spirit of evil."

Valar: "The great ones"; the fourteen Ainur who took physical form and chose to enter the world in order to fulfill a vision.

Valinor: The land where the Valar settled after the destruction of the lamps.

Vána (*vaa na*): One of the seven queens of the Valar; younger sister of Yavanna.

Vanyar: The first and smallest of the Elves.

Yavanna (*ya vaan na*): One of the seven queens of the Valar.

Gaelic

The *r*'s should have a slight roll.

Boann (*bo un*): The water spirit/goddess after whom the River Boyne is named; she is also known as the queen of the Formorians, a race that invaded Ireland.

Cerridwen (*ker eh dwen*): Dark Mother aspect of the Goddess.

Dagda (*dad ah*): The Father of All and Lord of Wisdom of the Tuatha de Danann.

Dana/Danu (*dawn ah*): The primary great Goddess who fulfills the dual role of Goddess/God; she is the "mother" of the Tuatha de Danann.

Lir (*leer*): Celtic sea god.

Lugh (*loo*): The Sun God whose father was of the Tuatha de Danann and mother of the Formorians, a race that arrived in Ireland during the time of the Tuatha de Danann.

Lughnasadh (*loo na sah*): The August 1 sabbat that honors Lugh and celebrates the early harvest.

Mabon (*may bone*): The autumn equinox.

Manannan (*manna ahn*): Son of Lir; as such he is also called Manannan mac Lir.

Ogham (*oh gom / oh yam*): Celtic runiclike writing.

Samhain (*sow en / sav in*): The sabbat honoring ancestors and other loved ones who have passed beyond the veil that separates the realms.

Sídhe (*shee*): The faeries.

Tir-na-nog (*teer nah nok*): Celtic version of the Land of the Dead where souls wait to be reborn; it is a land were one reverts to and retains his or her youth.

Tuatha de Danann (*too ah day thane nan*): In the mythological cycle of Ireland they are the fourth of five races to invade the island.

Latin

The *r*'s should have a slight roll.

Fons et origo (*fons eht oree go*): Source of all possible existence.

Meridians (*mer id ee ens*): South.

Septentrio (*sep ten tree o*): North.

Occidens (*ahk eh dens*): West.

Oriens (*ah ree ens*): East.

Tempus vernum (*tem pis ver num*): Springtime.

How to Make a flower Sachet

Materials

- **Fabric.** Look for something that is appropriate for the purpose, such as a simple cotton cloth with a flower design and soft or pastel colors. You may also want to look for fabric with a faery design.

- **Ribbon or yarn.** Look for a color that complements the colors of the fabric you choose. If you use ribbon, buy the very narrow ⅛-inch-wide ribbon. If it is wider it is more difficult to tie the little sachets.

You may want to get several fabric designs and colored ribbon/yarn for variety.

Assembling

- Cut four-inch squares, one for each sachet. Neatly trim the edges so they do not fray.

- Cut the ribbon or yarn into twelve- or thirteen-inch lengths.

- Place the square facing down—the good design side down—and then place three morning glory seeds and three moon flower seeds in the middle.

Figure D1—Flower sachet

- Carefully pick it up and gather the sides of the square together above the seeds.

- Wrap the ribbon/yarn around this gathered area and tie a knot to hold the sachet closed.

- Make a small bow over the knot, and it's done.

APPENDIX E

Preparing for Ritual

In addition to personal preparation (bathing/dressing/personal adornment) for ritual, the place of ritual needs to be prepared to accommodate the sacred energy that will be engaged. Even if you are going to be outdoors, the energy of place should be "cleansed" of potential negativity that could influence your circle. Some people use "smudging" once the circle is cast to cleanse both place and participants. There are various ways to cleanse and if you have one with which you are comfortable, continue to use it.

The preparation I offer is done in two stages: cleanse place first before setting up for ritual, and then when participants have gathered, use a "centering" exercise to bring everyone's energies into balance. Both incorporate the four elements.

Cleansing Place

You will need a small cup of saltwater and a stick of incense. To prepare the saltwater, I like to start with springwater and warm it slightly on the stove (to more easily dissolve the salt). Use a teaspoon of salt, not sea salt. Salt that is mined from the ground will represent the element earth. The saltwater embodies earth and water; the incense, fire and air. Together they represent the physical and ethereal; above and below.

Before setting up for ritual, walk around the perimeter of the area you plan to use. Light the incense and hold it in the same hand that you hold the cup of saltwater. As you walk and the incense trails behind you, lightly sprinkle saltwater over the area as you say:

> By earth and water, clear this quarter,
> By fire and air, make all fair.

Balancing Body

Close your eyes and take a deep breath. Release any tension. Become aware of your feet on the ground. Think of your energy extending below this floor, below this building to Mother Earth. Feel the solid foundation of earth that extends thousands of miles below you. The earth nourishes us, the earth cradles us.

Begin to draw this energy up into your body. Feel your legs heavy and solid with earth energy. As you continue to draw the energy up into your abdomen—the center of your sexuality, the source of life-giving moisture—feel the energy lighten into water. Continue to draw the energy up to your chest, to your heart where we think of spirit and love. Feel the spark of fire energy burn with the passion of life. As the energy continues upward feel air energy, the power of mind and knowledge, surround your head.

Hold the sensation of all four elements for a moment, and then allow the energy to return to Mother Earth, taking all negativity and tension from you.

You may also want to use the following as a prelude to ritual:

> We have come here from different places, different points in our lives. It is time to slow down, take a deep breath, and relax. Just as people have done for thousands of years and in thousands of ways, we gather in a circle for community and strength.
>
> Coming into ritual is a time of sharing, of giving and receiving. It is a time to go both within ourselves and outside of ourselves. It is a time to raise awareness of the energy of life that flows within our bodies, and it is a time to connect with the universal energy that flows everywhere around us. It is a time when we both direct the energy and get out of its way to let it flow naturally through us.

Bibliography

Books

Baggott, Andy. *Celtic Wisdom*. London: Piatkus Publishers, Ltd., 1999.

Cunningham, Scott. *Encyclopedia of Magical Herbs*. St. Paul, MN: Llewellyn Publications, 1998.

Ellis, Peter Berresford. *The Chronicles of the Celts*. New York: Carroll & Graf Publishers, Inc., 1999.

Ferguson, Diana. *The Magickal Year: A Pagan Perspective on the Natural World*. London: Labyrinth Publishing, 1996.

Fisher, Elizabeth. *Rise Up and Call Her Name*. Boston: Unitarian Universalist Women's Federation, 1994.

Foster, Robert. *The Complete Guide to Middle-Earth*. New York: Ballantine Books, 2001.

Graves, Robert. *The White Goddess: A Historical Grammar of Poetic Myth*. New York: The Noonday Press / Farrar, Straus and Giroux, 1975.

Kear, Katherine. *Flower Wisdom: The Definitive Guidebook to the Myth, Magic and Mystery of Flowers*. London: Thorsons, 2000.

Marks, Kate, comp. *Circle of Song: Songs, Chants and Dances for Ritual and Celebration*. Amherst, MA: Full Circle Press, 1993.

Matthews, Caitlin, and John Matthews. *Encyclopedia of Celtic Wisdom: A Celtic Shaman's Sourcebook*. Rockport, MA: Element Books, Inc., 1994.

McCoy, Edain. *Witta: An Irish Pagan Tradition*. St. Paul, MN: Llewellyn Publications, 1993.

O'Donohue, John. *Eternal Echoes.* New York: HarperCollins Publishers, 1995.

Pepper, Elizabeth, and John Wilcock. *The Witches' Almanac.* Newport, RI: The Witches' Almanac Ltd., 1996.

Pyne, Stephen J. *Vestal Fire.* Seattle, WA: University of Washington Press, 1997.

Redmond, Layne. *When the Drummers Were Women: A Spiritual History of Rhythm.* New York: Three Rivers Press, 1997.

Simmons, Philip. "Learning to Fall." *World Magazine,* May/June 1998, 26.

Tolkien, J. R. R. *The Book of Lost Tales 1.* Edited by Christopher Tolkien. New York: Ballantine Books, 1983.

———. *The Lord of the Rings.* New York: Houghton Mifflin Company, 1994.

———. *Unfinished Tales of Númenor and Middle-Earth.* New York: Houghton Mifflin Company, 1980.

Wolfe, Amber. *Elemental Power.* St. Paul, MN: Llewellyn Publications, 2001.

Audio

McKennitt, Loreena. *Parallel Dreams.* Ontario, Canada: Quinlan Road Limited, 1994. CD.

Starhawk and Reclaiming. *Chants: Ritual Music.* San Francisco: Reclaiming, 1987. Audiocassette.

———. *Second Chants: More Ritual Music from Reclaiming & Friends.* San Francisco: Reclaiming, 1994. Audiocassette.

Websites

http://www.chinesefortunecalendar.com/yinyang.htm
This site explains how the yin-yang symbol was developed.

http://www.dcs.ed.ac.uk/misc/local/TolkLang/pronlo/pronguide.html
This site provides a comprehensive guide to Elvish pronunciation.

Index